Java
Made Simple

P.K. McBride

MADE SIMPLE
BOOKS

Made Simple
An imprint of Butterworth-Heinemann
Linacre House, Jordan Hill, Oxford OX2 8DP
225 Wildwood Avenue, Woburn, MA 01801-2041
A division of Reed Educational and Professional Publishing Ltd

A member of the Reed Elsevier plc group

OXFORD   AUCKLAND   BOSTON
JOHANNESBURG   MELBOURNE   NEW DELHI

First published 1997
Reprinted 1998, 1999, 2000, 2001

British Library Cataloguing in Publication Data
A catalogue record for this book is available from the British Library

ISBN 0 7506 3241 0

Typeset by P.K.McBride, Southampton

Archtype, Bash Casual, Cotswold and Gravity fonts from Advanced Graphics Ltd
Icons designed by Sarah Ward © 1994
Printed and bound in Great Britain by Scotprint

FOR EVERY TITLE THAT WE PUBLISH, BUTTERWORTH-HEINEMANN
WILL PAY FOR BTCV TO PLANT AND CARE FOR A TREE.

Contents

Preface

Java is a new programming language, designed for use on networks – especially the Internet. The same Java code can be downloaded and run, without change, on a Sun workstation running Unix, a PC running DOS or Windows, or on an Apple Mac. To date it has mainly been used to create 'applets' on Web pages, but is now also being used to write full-scale applications.

The language is based upon C++, and is very similar in its style and structures. It is a large and wordy language. Gaining full proficiency in it must take time – if only because of the amount to be learned. However, its structures do follow a clear pattern, so that once the essentials have been mastered, it is relatively easy to extend one's knowledge.

This is book is not intended for proficient C++ programmers who want to transfer to Java – there are plenty of other books already on the shelves that do that job. It is aimed at those people who have little or no prior experience of programming, and it starts from scratch. I have concentrated on the basic concepts and practical uses of the language, and tried to avoid getting bogged down in technicalities. Purists may object to some over-simplifications – I hope you will appreciate them!

Java Made Simple will take you through to the point where you can write small applets for your Web pages, and give you the foundations and the confidence to go further into the language, if you wish to develop larger applications. Each feature is demonstrated at work in an applet or a short program, as new concepts are best learnt through practical examples. You will find exercises at the end of each chapter – use them to test your knowledge and to experiment with new ideas.

The text files for the larger programs, and for all of the answers to the exercises, can be found on the Made Simple Programming Web pages at the Butterworth-Heinemann site, at:

    http://www.bh.com

Good luck, and remember that Java gets its name from the coffee that you stop for whenever your brain hurts.

P.K.McBride, July 1997

1 Introducing Java

What is Java?

Java is a platform-independent, object-oriented, multi-threading, dynamically-linked programming language – and it has a lot of jargon. I'll try to keep the jargon to a minimum, but some is unavoidable. With that it mind, I'll try to answer the 'What is Java?' question again.

Java is the new programming language developed by Sun Microsystems, primarily for use on the World Wide Web. It has a lot in common with C++, so if you are competent in that language, you are well on the way to understanding Java. This book does not assume that you know anything about C++, or any other programming language, though a familiarity with Windows and a Web browser is assumed.

What can you do with Java?

With Java, you can produce three distinct types of programs – *applets, applications* and *beans*.

Applets are programs embedded into the HTML documents that form Web pages. Typically, they are small – so that someone browsing the Web does not have to wait long to download them. They will normally serve a limited purpose. Applets may provide a slicker means of navigating round a Web site, produce attention-grabbing animations, or simply entertain to encourage visitors to return regularly. They can also be used for more serious work. Plain Web pages are good for display but allow only limited feedback. Applets add true on-line interaction with the visitor – an insurance business, for example, could use applets to calculate instant quotes.

Applications are free-standing programs. You could use Java to write a wordprocessor, a spreadsheet, a graphics utility – in fact, any kind of application. Part of the Java grand design is the idea that it should be used to create applications for networked computers. Instead of installing standard software on individual PCs in a network, you would install Java applications on a central server, and download them into small networked computers for use during a session. It would allow simpler – and far cheaper – upgrading, as each application would only need installing once for the whole office. Java-using networked computers are still in their very early stages.

These applications would be modular. Instead of a 30+Mb all-singing, all-dancing wordprocessor, you would have a small editing module, and separate modules for spell-checking, layout, printing, etc, which could be downloaded – quickly – as needed. This approach allows the use of smaller, cheaper computers, and could simplify the production of software as the same modules could be reused in different applications – for example, the printing module could print documents from a wordprocessor or a spreadsheet.

Beans are a new addition to the Java package. They take the modular approach further. The concept here is that a bean should perform a specific, limited function, that could be called upon by other beans, applets or applications.

What do you need to learn?

To get started programming in Java, you need to understand:

- a few core concepts about programming in general and Object Oriented programming in particular (see the next few pages);

- how to set up your system for Java (later in this chapter);

- the basic structure of applications and applets (Chapter 2);

- how to store data in a program (Chapter 3);

- how to get the program to repeat actions or to perform them only if certain conditions are met (Chapter 4);

- the techniques for using Java's routines and structures in programs – and most of the rest of the book is given over to exploring a small part of what is a vast system.

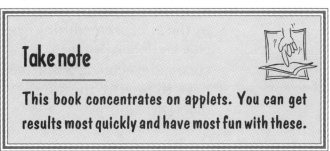

Take note

This book concentrates on applets. You can get results most quickly and have most fun with these.

Programming languages

A computer can only understand one language, and that is *machine code*. This consists of (binary) numbers that the chip translates into instructions, values and memory addresses. The instructions are extremely simple; e.g. 'move this value into memory at this address', 'compare these numbers', 'increment this value'.

There was a time when people wrote programs in machine code, but no-one in their right mind does it now – it's very hard work and there are better ways to write software.

Most programming languages use words and structures that are (more or less) comprehensible to humans. The programmer writes sequences of instructions as a text file – known as the *source code* – which must then be converted into machine code for the computer. Up until Java, there have been two ways of doing this.

- Some programming languages are *compiled*. The source code is passed to a *compiler* program, which first checks the text for syntax errors, and if it finds any, stops and displays a list of errors. The programmer must sort them all out and produce error-free code before the compiler will go on to the next stage and turn the text into an executable program. This is a block of machine code and can only be run on the right sort of machine – normally the same type that it was compiled on.

  If you want to run the same program on different platforms, such as Windows PCs, OS/2 computers and Macintoshes, you can – in theory – take the source code across and recompile it. In practice, the code will normally need some rewriting because each machine tends to do some things in its own special ways.

- Source code can also be *interpreted*. Here, the code is processed by the *interpreter* during execution. Each line is taken in turn, checked for errors, then – if it's error-free – converted to machine code and executed. As with the compiled languages, you normally have to rewrite the source code to transfer a program to a different platform.

JavaScript, another new language for use in Web pages, is an interpreted version of Java. Its code can be embedded in Web pages and executed when the page is displayed in a browser. If you want to know more about JavaScript, look out for *JavaScript Made Simple*.

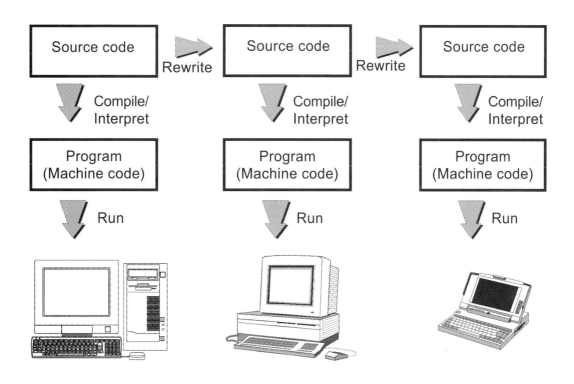

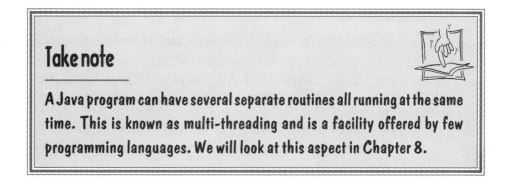

Take note

A Java program can have several separate routines all running at the same time. This is known as multi-threading and is a facility offered by few programming languages. We will look at this aspect in Chapter 8.

The Java Virtual Machine

With Java, Sun came up with a novel solution to the problem of how to allow one program to run on different platforms, and that is a neat piece of software called the Java Virtual Machine (or JVM). When you pass your Java source code to the Java compiler, it turns it into *byte code*. This is not machine code, but a half-way stage. Pass it to any computer that has the JVM installed, and this will read the byte code, convert it into machine code and run it.

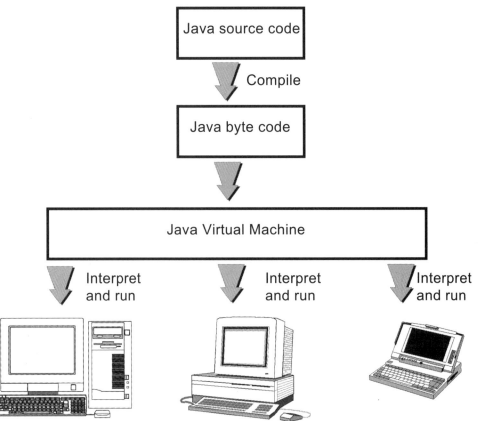

The main advantage of this approach is obvious. You can publish your program over the Internet knowing that any computer can run it, as long as it has the JVM. As this is built into Netscape and Internet Explorer, anyone using those browsers can run the same Java program.

The main disadvantage is less obvious. Because the JVM has to convert the byte code instructions to machine code before they can be executed, the program does not run as fast as a compiled program.

There is a also another disadvantage. A program is written specifically for one type of computer, can make full use of its facilities, optimising its speed, display, and use of peripherals. A program written for any (JVM) computer can only use those features that can be implemented on all. Sun Microsystems have got round this limitation by giving Java the ability to handle 'native code', i.e. code written specifically for one machine – which rather seems to take away the point...

JVM and your browser

If you have Netscape 2, 3 or 4, or Explorer 3, you have a Java Virtual Machine capable of running applets compiled under Java 1.0.

If you have Explorer 4, then your machine can also run applets compiled under Java 1.1 – the next Netscape will also handle these.

The Java Virtual Machine is an integral part of the browser software, and needs no installation, though you must turn on the Java-enabled option if you actually want to run applets!

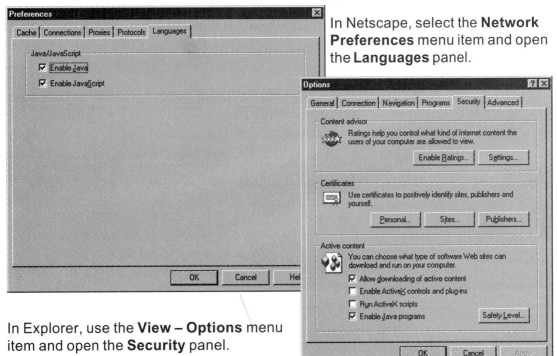

In Netscape, select the **Network Preferences** menu item and open the **Languages** panel.

In Explorer, use the **View – Options** menu item and open the **Security** panel.

Object Oriented programming

Java is an Object Oriented (OO) language. It's not the first, but is built on the firm foundations of earlier OO languages. The approach is now established as the way to do programming. You can – generally – produce better, more reliable programs faster with an Object Oriented language.

People write big books about the theory and practice of Object Oriented (OO) programming. I'm going to spend a couple of pages on it, which should be enough to give you a working grasp of its principles. We'll come back to it from time to time, as necessary.

Traditional v. OO languages

First, let's look at the difference between a 'traditional' programming language and an Object Oriented one. Think of a clickable button on a Windows screen. If you wanted to create this in a traditional language, you would have write some code to draw the button on the screen, then write some more to track the mouse movement (drawing the pointer) and watch for the click, and some more to draw the button as it is clicked, and then – at last – you can write the code to do the job called up by the click. Oh yes, and you'll have to do most of it again next time you want another clickable button!

Java, like most new Object Oriented languages, *knows* about buttons. It knows what they look like and how they interact with mice. If you want a clickable button in a Java program, all you have to do is specify where to put it, what to write on it, and what to do when it is clicked.

In an Object Oriented language, you have ready-made, reusable blocks of code – the objects.

The nature of objects

To understand the characteristics of objects, let's take an analogy from the real world. Think of a car. It has certain characteristics including its shape, colour, and speed and direction (when moving). In OO jargon, these are *variables*, some of which are set at the time of creation, and others which can be changed at any time.

With simple variables, you use expressions like this to change their values:

speed = 90

See Chapter 3

When working with objects, you use *methods* – built-in routines – to change the values held by its variables. This is a safety feature, ensuring that values are within acceptable ranges and that in changing one value you do not have unwanted effects on other aspects of the object. The method for changing the colour might look like this:

mycar.setColor(red);

In the jargon, we are sending a *message* to the **setColor** method of the **mycar** object, with the *parameter* **red**.

To go back to the analogy, if you want the car resprayed red, you could do it yourself, but you'd get a better result by taking it into a bodyshop. If you want to read the stockmarket reports in the paper and talk to your broker on the phone while you are travelling by car, you'd be safer with a chauffeur.

In OO jargon, this is called *encapsulation*. An object's variables are protected from direct contact with the outside world and can only be changed through the object's methods.

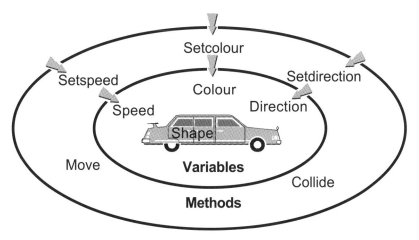

An object consists of variables and methods. Some methods are used for changing variables, others control its activities.

9

Objects and classes

When manufacturers are making cars, they does not design each one from scratch. Instead, they have a blueprint, and follow that – setting the colour, upholstery, engine size and other variables as required.

In OO jargon, the blueprint is called a *class*, and an object is an *instance* of a class. The process of creating a new object is called *instantiation*. (I never said the jargon was elegant.) The distinction between *class* and *object* gets a bit blurred, and here's why.

Inheritance

Let's look in on the design studio of the car manufacturer. Their new models will come in several versions – saloon, hatchback and estate, with a choice of 2-door or 4-door in each. They don't draw a new blueprint for each version. They start with a blueprint that covers the common elements, then adapt this to produce the basic saloon, hatchback and estate, and finally take each of those and develop the 2- and 4-door versions. After the first, each new blueprint inherits all the characteristics of its predecessor. It may adapt them slightly, and will add extra features of its own.

For an example of inheritance with objects and classes, let's look at the development of a simple database program for a car repair garage. The programmers have defined a simple record structure, to store the name, address, phone number and car model for each customer, along with methods to collect those details. This class is called **Owner** and can be used to create objects in which to store the customers' data. These might be called **Owner1**, **Owner2**, **Owner3**, etc.

If they want to cater for customers with a second car, they do not need to write another definition, but can create a new object of the **Owner** class, adding space for the second car. This might be called **RichOwner** – and it becomes a *class*, as it can be used to create new objects.

In the jargon, **RichOwner** is a *subclass* of **Owner** (and **Owner** is a *superclass* of **RichOwner**). The connection between the two continues after creation. If the **Owner** class is adapted to add date of last service, then that new field is added automatically to the **RichOwner** class.

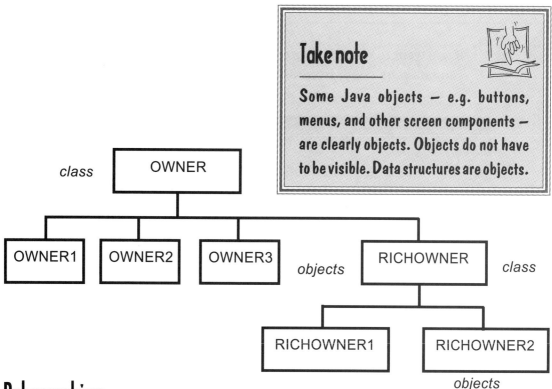

class   OWNER

OWNER1   OWNER2   OWNER3   *objects*   RICHOWNER   *class*

RICHOWNER1   RICHOWNER2

objects

Polymorphism

If Object Oriented programmers had been working on that car's blueprints, they could have produced a new blueprint (class) for each version; or incorporated all the variations within one master blueprint. This is *polymorphism* – the ability to create a new object in several different forms. For example, all of these are valid:

```
new rect = Rectangle()
new rect = Rectangle(50,100)
new rect = Rectangle(50,100,25,25)
```

The first creates a rectangle, 0 pixels high and wide, and at the top left of the screen – it's there ready to be grown and moved later. The second creates one 50 x 100 pixels, at the top left. The third creates one 50 x 100 pixels, 25 pixels down and right from the top left.

The message is the same in all cases – only the number of parameters changes. Technically this is achieved through having several methods with the same name but different definitions. The practical result is to give you much more flexibility.

The Java Development Kit

If you want to write Java programs, you need the development kit. You can get your copy, from JavaSoft at:

http://java.sun.com/products/jdk/

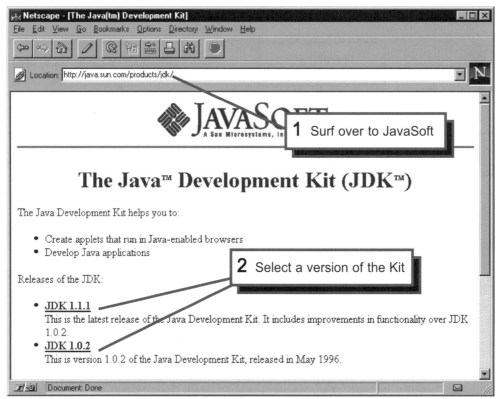

1 Surf over to JavaSoft

2 Select a version of the Kit

At the time of writing, there were two versions of the Kit – JDK 1.1.1 and JDK 1.0.2. By the time you read this, both will be available for Windows 95/NT, Sun Solaris and Macintosh machines.

- JDK 1.1.1 has features that cannot be run on the JVM in versions of Netscape and Internet Explorer – up to 3.0 of both. These replace and/or extend their equivalents in 1.0.2. You can avoid the newer features and compile your applets in 1.0.2 mode (see the Help files) if you want to reach the widest possible audience.

- At 3.7Mb, JDK 1.0.2 is less than half the size of the newer version. If you are short on space, or don't want to waste valuable download time, get this one, and upgrade when you need to.

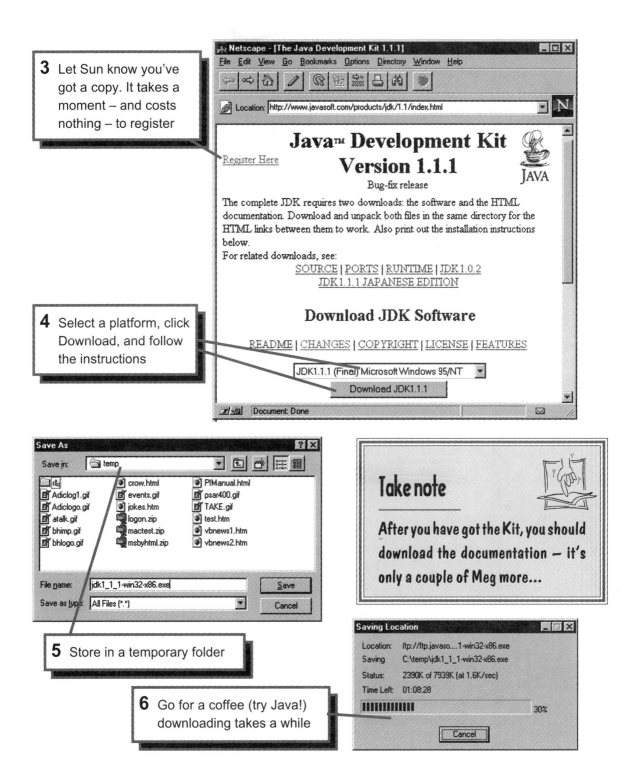

3 Let Sun know you've got a copy. It takes a moment – and costs nothing – to register

Netscape - [The Java Development Kit 1.1.1]

File Edit View Go Bookmarks Options Directory Window Help

Location: http://www.javasoft.com/products/jdk/1.1/index.html

Register Here

Java™ Development Kit Version 1.1.1

Bug-fix release

The complete JDK requires two downloads: the software and the HTML documentation. Download and unpack both files in the same directory for the HTML links between them to work. Also print out the installation instructions below.

For related downloads, see:

SOURCE | PORTS | RUNTIME | JDK1.0.2
JDK1.1.1 JAPANESE EDITION

Download JDK Software

README | CHANGES | COPYRIGHT | LICENSE | FEATURES

4 Select a platform, click Download, and follow the instructions

JDK1.1.1 (Final) Microsoft Windows 95/NT

Download JDK1.1.1

Document: Done

Save As

Save in: temp

r&i
Adiclog1.gif
Adiclogo.gif
atalk.gif
bhimp.gif
bhlogo.gif

crow.html
events.gif
jokes.htm
logon.zip
mactest.zip
msbyhtml.zip

PlManual.html
psar400.gif
TAKE.gif
test.htm
vbnews1.htm
vbnews2.htm

File name: jdk1_1_1-win32-x86.exe   Save

Save as type: All Files (*.*)   Cancel

5 Store in a temporary folder

Take note

After you have got the Kit, you should download the documentation – it's only a couple of Meg more...

Saving Location

Location: ftp://ftp.javaso....1-win32-x86.exe
Saving   C:\temp\jdk1_1_1-win32-x86.exe
Status: 2390K of 7939K (at 1.6K/sec)
Time Left: 01:08:28

30%

Cancel

6 Go for a coffee (try Java!) downloading takes a while

Upacking the Kit

The Java Development Kit comes as a self-extracting zip file, with a in-built installation routine. All you need to do is click the mouse button a couple of times and make a couple of choices.

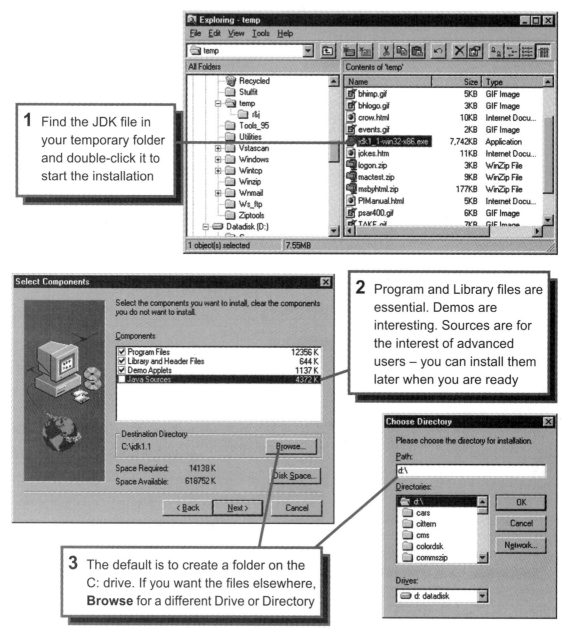

1 Find the JDK file in your temporary folder and double-click it to start the installation

2 Program and Library files are essential. Demos are interesting. Sources are for the interest of advanced users – you can install them later when you are ready

3 The default is to create a folder on the C: drive. If you want the files elsewhere, **Browse** for a different Drive or Directory

The Kit parts

The JDK consists of a number of tools and supporting files, including:

The compiler (javac.exe)

This converts the text files of your Java programs (the source code) into Java byte code. In the Windows version, this, like all the tools, is a DOS program and is best run from the MS-DOS prompt. *See page 20.*

The interpreter (java.exe)

This will take the byte code of a java *application* – not an *applet* – and execute it. Though we will not be developing any serious applications in this book, we will be using them to test methods and techniques. It is simpler to test applications than applets. *See page 20.*

The appletviewer (appletviewer.exe)

This is a small window in which you can view an HTML page containing an applet. Most of the time you can view applets more conveniently in your browser, though you will need it for those that use the 1.1 features if your browser cannot handle these. *See pages 24 and 82.*

The decompiler (javap.exe)

This will take a compiled program and convert it into a Java text file. Use this when you come across the Java bytecode of a finished applet and want to know how it was written. If the applet was called 'finished.class', then this command line would generate the text file:

```
javap finished.class finished.java
```

The documentation

The JDK includes a mass of help pages. These are all HTML documents and are stored within the DOCS\GUIDE folder. *See page 26.*

Other files

Amongst these are several tools, such as the debugger, for advanced users. When you are ready for these, try *Java: A Practical Approach* by Neil Fawcett & Terry Ridge, also from by Butterworth-Heinemann.

Getting ready

Windows users have three jobs to do at the start of each session.

- Set the **PATH**. *A* path is the position of a file in the hierarchy of folders. *The* PATH is the list of folders that Windows searches when it needs a file to run a program – if the file isn't in the current folder. The PATH normally includes C: and \WINDOWS amongst others – it depends on what other software you have installed. The Java tools are stored in the JDK\BIN folder, so this must be added to the PATH if you want to use them while you are in another folder.

- Set the **CLASSPATH**. This is similar to the Windows PATH, and tells the Java system where to look for your programs and the CLASSES.ZIP file. Your programs will be in the current folder; CLASSES.ZIP is in your JDK\LIB folder.

- Switch to the folder in which you store your Java programs. This could be the top-level JDK folder, but it's better to create a new one for them. Mine is called FILES, and it's in the JDK folder.

The simplest way to do these is to create a short batch file. This is a list of DOS commands stored in a file with a .BAT extension. Batch files are run from the MS-DOS prompt, but you must start that up anyway, to run the Java compiler and interpreter.

Create this short file in Notepad, adjusting the paths to the JDK and working folders to suit your setup.

```
SET PATH=%PATH%;C:\JDK1.1\BIN
SET CLASSPATH = .;C:\JDK1.1\LIB\CLASSES.ZIP
CD\JDK1.1\FILES
```

- The first line takes the existing PATH settings (%PATH%) and adds the \BIN folder to it.

- The second lists the current folder (.) and the CLASSES.ZIP path.

- The third line moves you to your working folder.

Save the file in your \WINDOWS folder (or anywhere else in the existing PATH) as GOJAVA.BAT.

At the start of a session, run the MS-DOS prompt and type 'GOJAVA'.

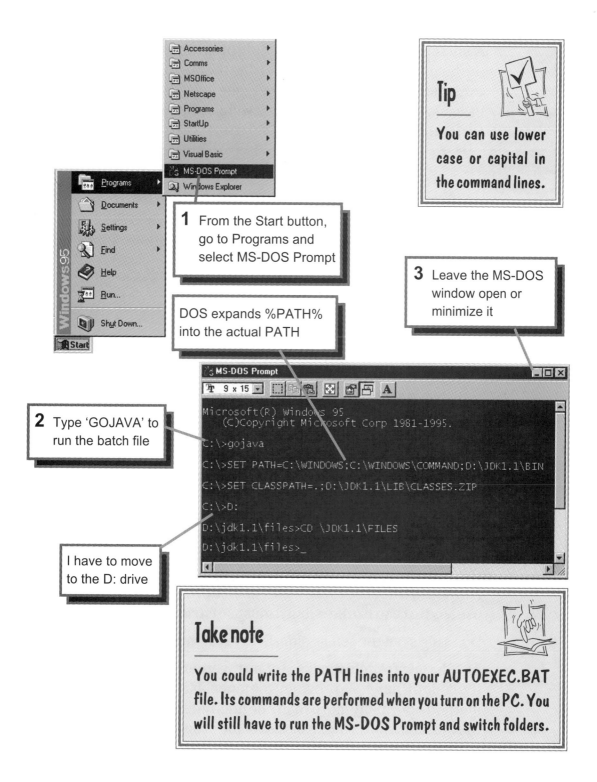

Accessories ▶
Comms ▶
MSOffice ▶
Netscape ▶
Programs ▶
StartUp ▶
Utilities ▶
Visual Basic ▶
MS-DOS Prompt
Windows Explorer

Programs ▶
Documents ▶
Settings ▶
Find ▶
Help
Run...
Shut Down...

Start

Windows 95

Tip

You can use lower case or capital in the command lines.

1 From the Start button, go to Programs and select MS-DOS Prompt

3 Leave the MS-DOS window open or minimize it

DOS expands %PATH% into the actual PATH

MS-DOS Prompt

T 9 x 15

```
Microsoft(R) Windows 95
   (C)Copyright Microsoft Corp 1981-1995.

C:\>gojava

C:\>SET PATH=C:\WINDOWS;C:\WINDOWS\COMMAND;D:\JDK1.1\BIN

C:\>SET CLASSPATH=.;D:\JDK1.1\LIB\CLASSES.ZIP

C:\>D:

D:\jdk1.1\files>CD \JDK1.1\FILES

D:\jdk1.1\files>_
```

2 Type 'GOJAVA' to run the batch file

I have to move to the D: drive

Take note

You could write the PATH lines into your AUTOEXEC.BAT file. Its commands are performed when you turn on the PC. You will still have to run the MS-DOS Prompt and switch folders.

17

The first application

A Java application is a free-standing program that can be run – with the help of the Java Interpreter – from the MS-DOS Prompt. This first example is about as small as they come, but it is enough to show the basic shape of a Java application. It will also be enough to test that you system is working correctly.

```
class Hello
{
    public static void main(String[] args)
    {
        System.out.println("Hello from Java");
    }
}
```

Let's take it a line at a time.

```
class Hello
```

A Java program is a class. Every class has a name, and the convention is that a class name starts with a capital letter.

```
public static void main(String[] args)
```

This is the first line in all applications. Java applications must have a method called **main**, which is where execution starts. **public** makes the application accessible from outside, i.e. from MS-DOS. We'll come back to this and look at the rest of that line later.

```
System.out.println("Hello from Java");
```

A program consists of a number of statements (instructions) – in this case, only one. It uses the **println** method (part of the **out** section of the **System** object) to display a message on the screen. The **ln** at the end does a Line Feed to push the cursor down to the next line. You can use any text you like here, but it must be enclosed in "double quotes".

Don't miss out the semi-colon. Every statement must end with one.

The {brackets} hold blocks of code together. The outer pair enclose the code of the whole program; the inner pair enclose that of the **main** method – normally more than one line! Indenting the code between the brackets shows the structure of the program, but is not essential.

Start your text editor or wordprocessor and type in the text – exactly as give here. Correct use of capitals and punctuation is crucial.

Save the file as a Text document and call it "Hello.java". Again, notice the capital letter. The filename must be the same as the class name and must have the '.java' extension.

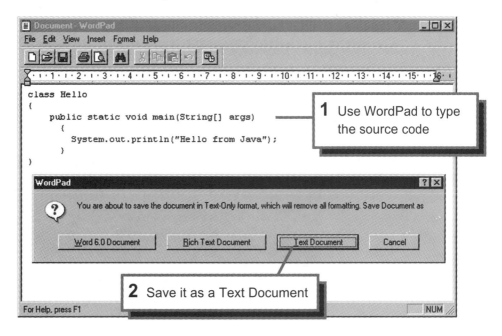

Which wordprocessor?

WordPad is ideal for this job. You don't need the facilities of a full-blown wordprocessor, and Notepad can handle only very small files – you'd be surprised how your programs grow! WordPad also has the recently used files listed on its File menu. When you are switching between programs – or between applet and HTML code (see page 22) – it is very handy to be able to pick them off here.

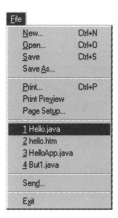

Move to the MS-DOS Prompt and type:

    javac Hello.java

This should compile the program and produce a file called 'Hello.class'. If the compiler find any errors, it will tell you what they are and which line they are on. If it does, read the message to find out what they are, edit the text file and try again.

To run the application, pass it to the Java interpreter with:

    java Hello

Notice that you use exactly the same program name, but without any extension this time. You should see your text displayed on the screen.

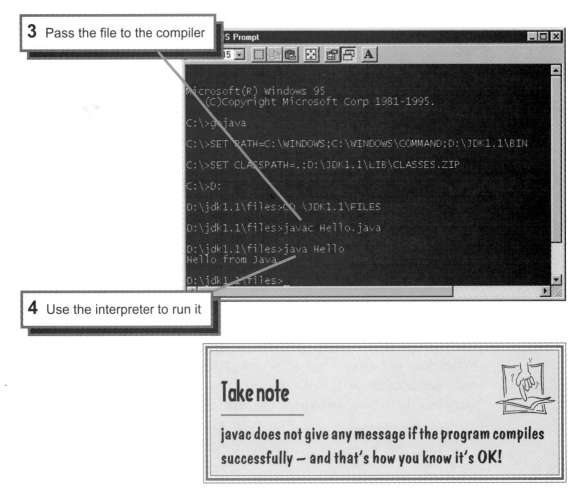

3 Pass the file to the compiler

```
Microsoft(R) Windows 95
    (C)Copyright Microsoft Corp 1981-1995.

C:\>go java

C:\>SET PATH=C:\WINDOWS;C:\WINDOWS\COMMAND;D:\JDK1.1\BIN

C:\>SET CLASSPATH=.;D:\JDK1.1\LIB\CLASSES.ZIP

C:\>D:

D:\jdk1.1\files>CD \JDK1.1\FILES

D:\jdk1.1\files>javac Hello.java

D:\jdk1.1\files>java Hello
Hello from Java

D:\jdk1.1\files>
```

4 Use the interpreter to run it

Take note

javac does not give any message if the program compiles successfully – and that's how you know it's OK!

The first applet

Now let's test the rest of the system. Again, this is about as small as you can get a working applet, though this time you will also have to create an HTML document, to provide a home for the applet.

The source code

Type in the following code. Like the first application, this displays a message, but does it in a different way – applets run within browsers, and that has an impact on everything to do with the screen display.

```
import java.applet.Applet;
import java.awt.Graphics;

public class HelloApp extends Applet
{
    public void paint(Graphics g)
    {
        g.drawString("Hello from an applet!", 50, 20);
    }
}
```

1 Type in the code for the applet

Let's see what this does.

```
import java.applet.Applet;
import java.awt.Graphics;
```

Applets are objects derived from the **Applet** class, one of the **java.applet** group of classes. All screen display is done through objects derived from the **Graphics** class, in the **java.awt** (Abstract Windows Toolkit) set. To be able to use these classes, we must bring the code into our program with the **import** command. You'll have to import different classes depending upon the jobs you want your program to do. You will always need **java.applet.Applet**, and normally need one or more classes from the **java.awt** set.

```
public class HelloApp extends Applet
```

This is where the applet really starts. The code is made public, so it can be executed, and given its class name. You've already seen that names should start with a capital. The convention is that, where names are constructed from several words, each starts with a capital.

```
public void paint(Graphics g)
```

Screen display is normally done from within **paint()**, using different methods for drawing, setting colours and writing text, all of which are part of the **Graphics** class. We will be exploring many of these later.

```
g.drawString("Hello from an applet!", 50, 20);
```

drawString is one of the methods that will put words on the screen. It takes three *parameters*, or values. The text, the number of pixels from the left (**x** co-ordinate) and the number from the top (**y** co-ordinate).

As with applications, {brackets} are used here to enclose blocks of code, and again, these can be indented to make the structure clearer.

Save the file as a Text document, and call it 'HelloApp.java'.

Go to the MS-DOS Prompt and compile the applet:

```
javac HelloApp.java
```

If you get any error messages, read them, edit the text and try again.

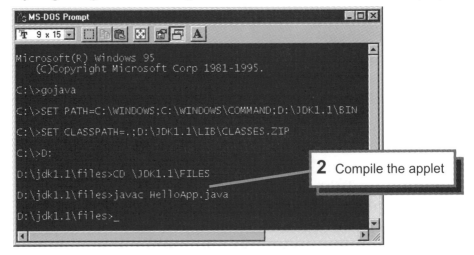

The HTML document

The only way that you can run an applet is from within an HTML document. So, start a new document and type in the code opposite. If you don't know how to write HTML, just copy in the code carefully – take special care that where you have a pair of matching tags, like **<BODY>** and **</BODY>**, there is a /slash at the start of the second one.

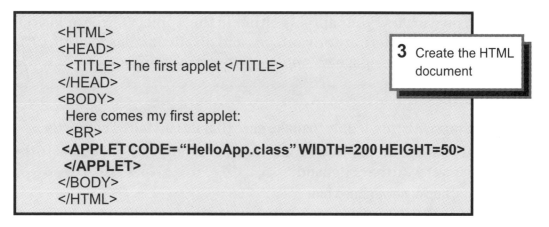

```
<HTML>
<HEAD>
 <TITLE> The first applet </TITLE>
</HEAD>
<BODY>
 Here comes my first applet:
 <BR>
<APPLET CODE= "HelloApp.class" WIDTH=200 HEIGHT=50>
 </APPLET>
</BODY>
</HTML>
```

3 Create the HTML document

The only HTML we have room for here, are those bits relating to applets. Here are the crucial two lines again.

```
<APPLET CODE= "HelloApp.class" WIDTH=200 HEIGHT=50>
</APPLET>
```

The **<APPLET...>** and **</APPLET>** tags mark the start and end of code that handles the applet. In this case, there is the absolute minimum of information between them, but the applet code can run to several lines as you will see later (Chapter 5).

CODE = "HelloApp.class" tells the browser which file to run.

WIDTH = 200 HEIGHT = 50 defines the size (in pixels) of the area in which to run the applet. It shows up on screen as a grey rectangle. The applet area can be any size you like.

When you have got the HTML code typed in, and checked, save the file as a Text document, calling it 'hello.htm'. You can use lower case or capitals with HTML files – it doesn't matter.

Tip

If you want to learn about HTML, you might like to try *Designing Internet Home Pages Made Simple*.

Viewing applets

You can view your applets either in the AppletViewer or in your browser. There are advantages and disadvantages to both. (*The AppletViewer*, page 82, *Applets in the browser*, page 84.)

The AppletViewer

Start with this, if only to make sure that it is installed correctly.

Go back to the MS-DOS Prompt and pass the HTML document to the viewer with the command:

    appletviewer hello.htm

You should see your applet displayed in the AppletViewer.

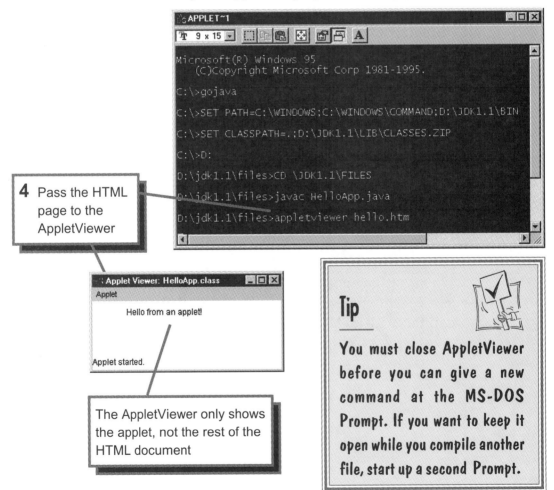

4 Pass the HTML page to the AppletViewer

The AppletViewer only shows the applet, not the rest of the HTML document

Tip

You must close AppletViewer before you can give a new command at the MS-DOS Prompt. If you want to keep it open while you compile another file, start up a second Prompt.

24

Using the browser

Run your browser and use its Open – File command to load in the 'hello.htm' file.

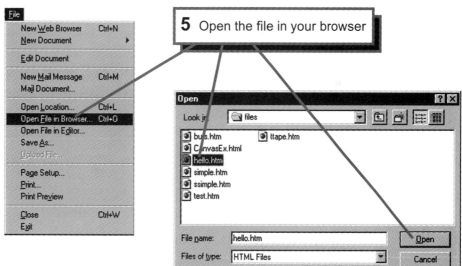

This should show the 'Here comes my first applet' text, followed by the applet, displayed on a grey background.

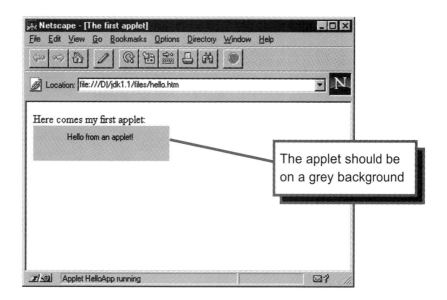

Exploring Java

One of the problems of Java is that it is a massive language. There are hundreds of classes – over 50 in the AWT (Abstract Windows Toolkit) alone – and literally thousands of fields and methods. Rather than trying to learn them all – a horrendous task – get to know your way around the documentation. Its explanations are brief and it lacks the examples that could clarify new concepts, but it does at least show you what is available. And there are common patterns of use for most of the classes and methods, so that once you have mastered one class or method, you can apply the techniques to other related ones.

1   If you haven't got the documentation, go and get it now from:

http://www.javasoft.com

You want **jdk1_1-docs_html.zip**. The file is just under 2Mb.

2   When you extract the files with WinZIP, select your java folder and make sure that the Use Folder Names option is selected. This will create the necessary folders and put all the files in the proper places.

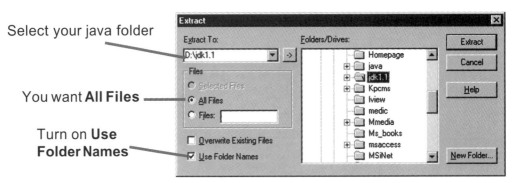

Select your java folder

You want **All Files**

Turn on **Use Folder Names**

3   In Windows Explorer, go to your **Java** folder and open first the **docs**, then the **guide** folders. There are 15 folders within **guide**, each covering a different aspect of the system, and each with its own **index.html** file. The one you will want to use most often is in **awt**. Open this in your browser.

4   The whole of the documentation is woven together with hypertext links. The **java.awt** package is a good place to start.

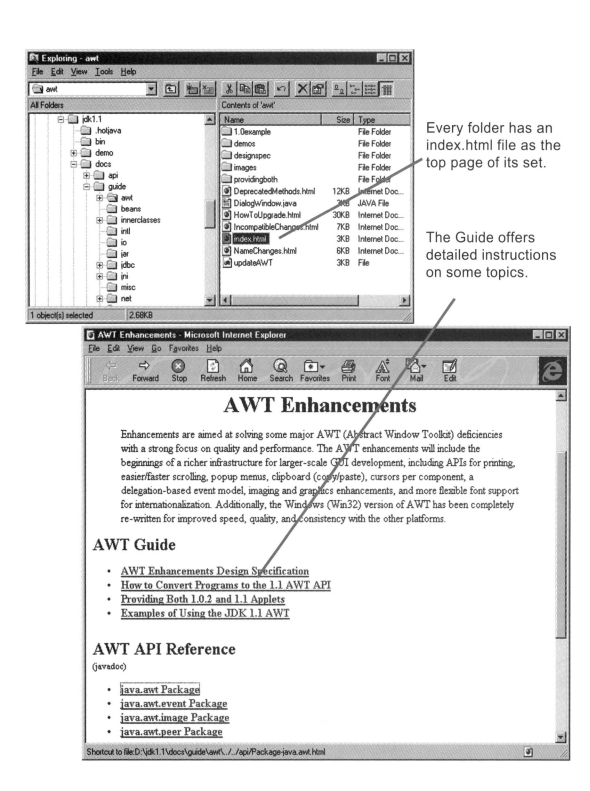

Every folder has an index.html file as the top page of its set.

The Guide offers detailed instructions on some topics.

These are the main
indexes for the guide

Interfaces provide
cross-links between
classes

Every class is
documented

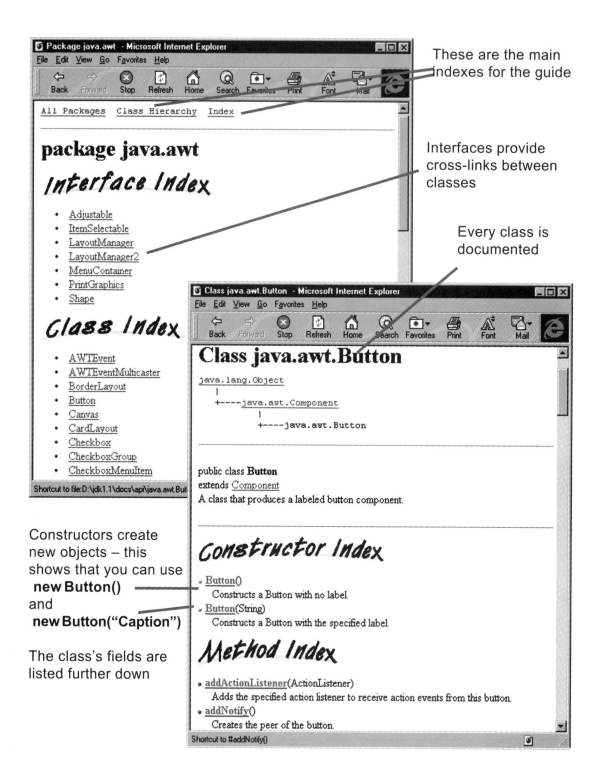

Constructors create
new objects – this
shows that you can use
new Button()
and
new Button("Caption")

The class's fields are
listed further down

The Index

This is an enormous file – over 1.4Mb – which does not make for ease of use. It takes several minutes to load into a browser, even on a fast machine, and if you browse on and then return to the page, it will take as long to reload! You can print it out, but it runs to over 200 pages and you will, of course, lose the hyperlinks.

Despite its size, it is not that hard to track down information in the Index. Java method names follow certain patterns. For instance, methods which assign values usually start '*set...*'; those which return values usually start '*get...*'. And names are descriptive, making keyword searches fruitful. If you wanted, say, to see what image-handling methods were available, setting the browser to find '*image*' would find most of the relevant methods.

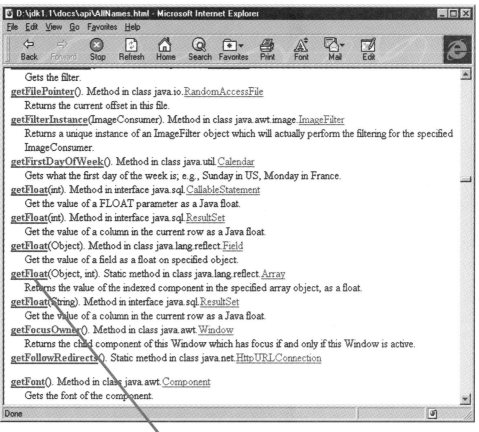

The links are mainly to the class pages

Exercises

1 Write and an application to display your name and address on the screen, with a separate line for each part of the address.

Don't forget to end each statement with a semi-colon.

Save it as "Address.java", compile and run it.

2 Repeat Exercise 1 as an applet, called "AddressApp.java". Position the text so that it is aligned to the right of the applet – expect to spend a little time experimenting with the co-ordinates to get this right!

Embed it in a Web page with the text: "Here's my address" above, and "Please write" below.

2 Variables and values

Data types

Variables are named places in memory where you can store the data needed in your programs. You can have as many variables as you need, and call them what you like – though there are certain rules and conventions for variable names (see page 34). When you compile your program, the system will allocate space for the variables, and convert the names into memory address (that the computer uses).

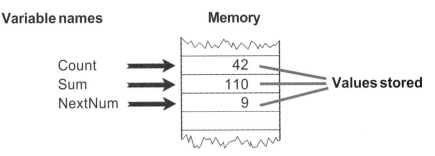

We'll return to variables shortly. First we must look at data types. Java recognises several data types, allocating different amounts of memory to each – the aim being not to use more than is necessary.

Primitive data types

These are the simplest types and are used for storing numbers, characters and Boolean values.

There are four formats for integers (whole numbers):

byte	-128 to + 127	(1 byte storage)
short	–32768 to + 32767	(2 bytes)
int	-2,147,483,648 to +2,147,483,647	(4 bytes)
long	+/- 9 billion billion!	(8 bytes)

And two for floating point numbers – those with decimal places. Both can cope with astronomical or microscopic values. The most significant difference is in the precision with which they store the numbers.

float	Accurate to 8 significant figures
double	Accurate to 16 significant figures

What this means is that if you calculated a float value to be 12345.6789123 it would actually be held as 12345.679.

Most programming languages can only handle ASCII characters, which is fine for limited (Western) character sets. Java uses Unicode encoding which can cope with character sets of up to 65,000 characters.

char   single character

Boolean values can only be either *true* or *false*. As you will see in Chapter 3, they are mainly used for carrying the results of a test from one part of a program to another.

Reference data types

When you create a variable of a primitive data type, you set up a named place in memory with just enough space to hold the value. This is fine with numbers and characters as they have a defined size. You cannot use the same approach with more complex data structures because the amount of storage space will vary from one item to another. How much space do you need for someone's name or address? How much space does an object take?

With a reference data type, the named space in memory does not hold the data. Instead it holds the *address* of where the data is stored. If you haven't done any programming before, you may find this a rather subtle distinction, but it has a crucial impact on how you handle variables of these types. You will see this when we start to use them.

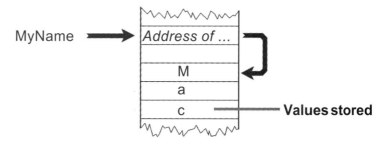

Reference data types include:

String and **stringBuffer**   for storing text (page 52)

Arrays   sets of variables of the same type (page 48)

Creating variables

Declaration

This is the process of setting up a variable. You tell the system the type and what you want to call it, like this:

```
int     Count;
float   Salary;
```

These declarations create an integer called Count, and a floating point variable called Salary. Notice that these lines, as with all commands, have a semi-colon at the end.

You can declare several variables of the same type in one line. Give the type at the start, and separate the variable names with commas.

```
int  startVal, currentVal, endVal;
```

Variables can be declared at any point in a program – as long as it is before you attempt to use them. Normal practice is to declare variables at the start of the program, or at the start of the block of code in which they are used. (But see *The scope of variables*, page 54.)

Variable names

Variable names must start with a letter, dollar sign ($) or underscore (_) and may contain any combination of letters and digits. Spaces cannot be used, and symbols (apart from _ and $) should be avoided.

You can use either upper or lower case letters in a name, but mix them with care as Java is case-sensitive. *myName*, *myname*, *MyName*, and *MYNAME* are four different things. The convention is to use capitals only at the start of following words in a multi-word name.

Keeping names reasonably short and simple will cut down typing errors, but perhaps the most important rule is to make sure that the names mean something to you!

```
int     age;
char    sex;
int     oldX, oldY, newX, newY;
double    taxPaidToDate;
```

Assigning values

You can assign a value to a variable when you declare it, like this:

```
type    variable = expression;
```

or assign a value later in the program, with the simpler statement:

```
variable = expression;
```

It doesn't matter which way you do it. If a variable is to have an initial value, you may as well assign it when you declare the variable.

The expression can be a literal value (a number, character or string of text), or a calculation or other operation that produces a value. The values should be of the same type as the variable, though you can give number variables values which are too large for the type – they are simply chopped down to fit.

Numbers can be given as octal, hexadecimal or exponential values, as well as in normal (denary) form. We'll stick to ordinary numbers, which will do all we want to do.

Single characters are given in single quotes, e.g. 'A'. If you should need to use ones from the Unicode system, it must be given as a hexadecimal value like this:

```
'\u01F2'
```

Strings of text are given in "double quotes".

These are valid assignments:

```
count = 42;
char    sex = 'M';
myName = "Fred";
```

Time to put this into practice. Type in this application source code. Save it as 'Vars1.java' and compile it with:

    javac Vars1.java

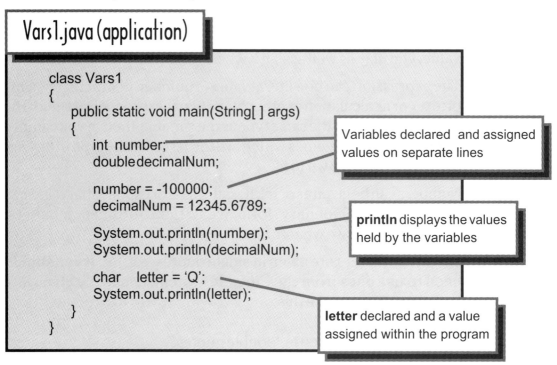

Vars1.java (application)

```
class Vars1
{
    public static void main(String[ ] args)
    {
        int  number;
        double decimalNum;

        number = -100000;
        decimalNum = 12345.6789;

        System.out.println(number);
        System.out.println(decimalNum);

        char    letter = 'Q';
        System.out.println(letter);
    }
}
```

Variables declared and assigned values on separate lines

println displays the values held by the variables

letter declared and a value assigned within the program

If you get any error messages, check them carefully and compare your code with mine – paying particular attention to punctuation and capital letters.

When it has compiled, run it with:

    java Vars1

The program should display the values held by the variables.

```
-100000
12345.6789
Q
```

Tip

Where you have similar lines, make full use of the Edit – Copy and Paste commands.

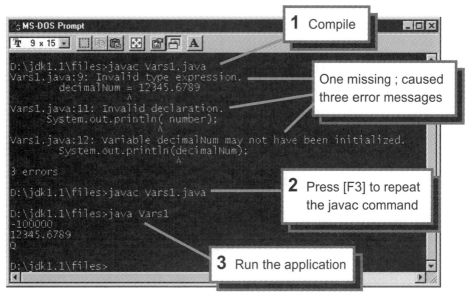

```
MS-DOS Prompt                                          _ □ ×
T  9 x 15 ▼  □ 🗐 🗎 ⊠ 🗎🗎 A
D:\jdk1.1\files>javac Vars1.java
Vars1.java:9: Invalid type expression.
        decimalNum = 12345.6789
                   ^
Vars1.java:11: Invalid declaration.
        System.out.println( number);
                          ^
Vars1.java:12: Variable decimalNum may not have been initialized.
        System.out.println(decimalNum);
                          ^
3 errors

D:\jdk1.1\files>javac Vars1.java

D:\jdk1.1\files>java Vars1
-100000
12345.6789
Q

D:\jdk1.1\files>
```

1 Compile

One missing ; caused three error messages

2 Press [F3] to repeat the javac command

3 Run the application

Common errors: No. 1

One of the most common errors is forgetting to put a semi-colon at the end of a statement. The error message that you get from this will not be a helpful 'Missing semi-colon'. The compiler will assume that the statement runs over onto the next line (which does finish with a semi-colon), try to make sense of it all, and tell you that you have errors on both lines. If – as happens in the screenshot example – the semi-colon is missing from the declaration, errors will also be found on every line that uses the variable.

Always tackle your errors from the top. In the example, curing the error on line 9 (the semi-colon) will also fix those on lines 11 and 12.

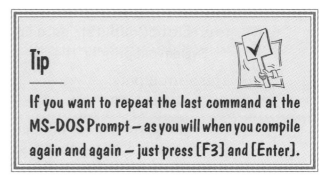

Tip

If you want to repeat the last command at the MS-DOS Prompt – as you will when you compile again and again – just press [F3] and [Enter].

Outputs

When you display a variable, you will normally display a message to tell the user what it is. The **println** method has two limitations:

- you can only display one item at a time;
- it does a line feed, forcing the cursor to the next line.

So, you could do this:

```
System.out.println("The score is ");
System.out.println(score);
```

but the display is not impressive:

```
The score is
29
```

There are two solutions to this.

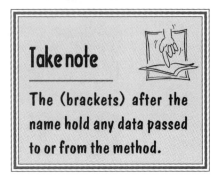

System.out.print

This method also displays values or variables on screen, but does not do a line feed at the end. If you want two or more items to appear in a continuous line, use a succession of **print**s, followed by a **println**.

```
System.out.print("The score is ");
System.out.println(score);
```

The output this time is:

```
The score is 29
```

Which definitely looks better – but you must remember to include a space at the end of your text, to separate it from the following item.

Combined outputs

You can combine any number of values, variables and literal strings to create one ouput string, using the + operator, e.g.

```
System.out.println("The score is "+ score);
```

This also outputs:

```
The score is 29
```

As a general rule, the combined string approach works best where there are a limited number of smallish items in the output line. The strings themselves can be thousands of characters long, but beyond a certain point, the combined expression becomes difficult to type correctly and to read, and it is easier to break the output down over several lines. Clarity is more important than compactness!

The next example demonstrates the combined approach, and also uses a few more data types. It is an extension of the last program – save a little time and typing by copying its code as a basis for this.

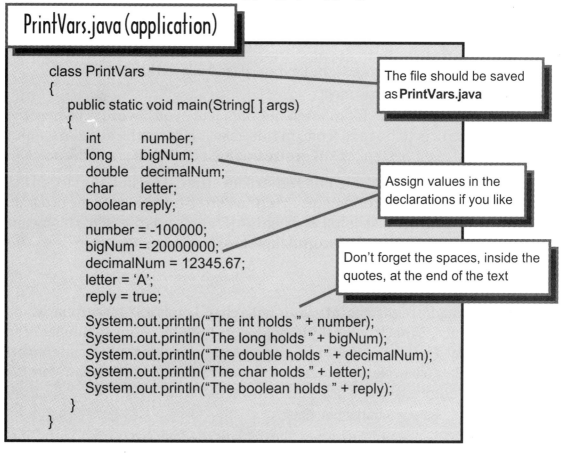

PrintVars.java (application)

```
class PrintVars
{
    public static void main(String[ ] args)
    {
        int       number;
        long      bigNum;
        double    decimalNum;
        char      letter;
        boolean   reply;

        number = -100000;
        bigNum = 20000000;
        decimalNum = 12345.67;
        letter = 'A';
        reply = true;

        System.out.println("The int holds " + number);
        System.out.println("The long holds " + bigNum);
        System.out.println("The double holds " + decimalNum);
        System.out.println("The char holds " + letter);
        System.out.println("The boolean holds " + reply);
    }
}
```

The file should be saved as **PrintVars.java**

Assign values in the declarations if you like

Don't forget the spaces, inside the quotes, at the end of the text

Your output should look like this:

```
The int holds number
The long holds bigNum
The double holds decimalNum
The char holds letter
The boolean holds reply
```

Inputs

There is, alas, no simple equivalent to **println** for getting keyboard input into a Java application. In practice, this does not matter if your aim is to write applets – there are (relatively) easy ways of getting input into applets! (See page 112.) However, you should at least know how to read a single character from the keyboard – you'll have to do this in a couple of example applications later in the book. The process also illustrates some fundamental points about the Java system.

System.in.read()

This method reads the keyboard, and is used like this:

```
a = System.in.read();
```

Notice that **read()** alone is not sufficient – you have to say where the data is to be read from. In this case it is from the standard input stream, **System.in**. Other streams include disk files and the ports.

The keyboard is a *buffered* stream – the data is initially stored in a special block of memory. It is transferred from there to the program when the buffer is full, or when the [Enter] key is pressed. This means that you cannot pick up a single keystroke directly.

Typecasting

read() returns an **int** value – not a **char**. Java is a 32-bit system, which means that it normally handles data in 32-bit chunks – the size of an int. Converting this to a char presents no problems. You can convert data from one type to another by *typecasting*. To do this, you write the required type, in brackets, in front of the data, e.g.:

```
letter = (char) input_data;
```

In the example program, the data is typecast as it is read, in the line:

```
c = (char)System.in.read();
```

Exceptions

Java is safety-conscious. Any method which may produce a fatal error must be protected by an error-trapping. In the Java jargon, this is known as *exception-handling*. Sometimes you will have to write your own routines in a program to deal with exceptions; other times you can pass them back to the Java system, and that will simply shut down the program safely. Here's the relevant line in this program:

```
throws java.io.IOException
```

Notice that it follows directly on from the **main()** line, and that there is no semi-colon before it or after it. It is essential – miss it out and the program will not compile.

We'll come back to exceptions as we need to, later in the book.

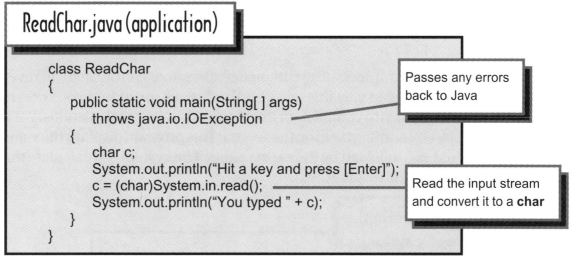

ReadChar.java (application)

```
class ReadChar
{
    public static void main(String[ ] args)
        throws java.io.IOException
    {
        char c;
        System.out.println("Hit a key and press [Enter]");
        c = (char)System.in.read();
        System.out.println("You typed " + c);
    }
}
```

Passes any errors back to Java

Read the input stream and convert it to a **char**

Compile it and run it. follow the prompt and you should see this:

```
Hit a key and press [Enter]
A
You typed A
```

Take note

There's more about Exceptions on page 76.

41

Calculations

In Java there are five arithmetic operators:

    +   addition
    −   subtraction
    *   multiplication
    /   division – how many times it goes
    %   division – remainder

Notice those last two. When you divide integers (on paper), you get two results – how many times, and the remainder. e.g.

    14 / 4 = 3 remainder 2

To get both values in Java, you must do two calculations:

    14 / 4 = 3   then   14 % 4 = 2

The values produced by arithmetic expressions can be used wherever you can use a variable or a literal value, e.g. print them on screen, assign them to variables, or use them within other calculations. We'll start by printing them on the screen. This program displays the sums (as text) followed by the expressions. The system will calculate the results and display them.

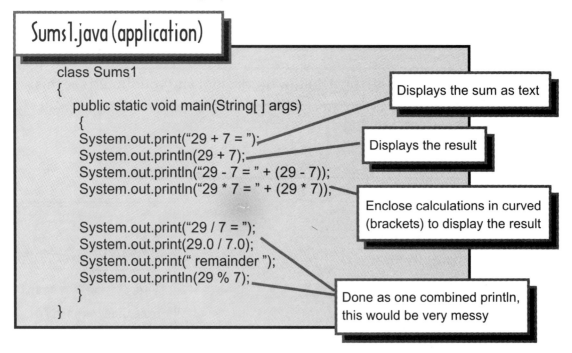

Sums1.java (application)

```
class Sums1
{
    public static void main(String[ ] args)
    {
    System.out.print("29 + 7 = ");
    System.out.println(29 + 7);
    System.out.println("29 - 7 = " + (29 - 7));
    System.out.println("29 * 7 = " + (29 * 7));

    System.out.print("29 / 7 = ");
    System.out.print(29.0 / 7.0);
    System.out.print(" remainder ");
    System.out.println(29 % 7);
    }
}
```

Displays the sum as text

Displays the result

Enclose calculations in curved (brackets) to display the result

Done as one combined println, this would be very messy

When compiled and executed, you should see this output:

```
29 + 7 = 36
29 - 7 = 22
29 * 7 = 203
29 / 7 = 4 remainder 1
```

That last program used integer values. See what happens with decimal fractions. Edit it to change 29 to 29.5, and 7 to 7.1. (If you are using WordPad, its Replace function will make this a simple job.) Compile again and run. This time you should see this:

```
29.5 + 7.1 = 36.6
29.5 - 7.1 = 22.4
29.5 * 7.1 = 209.45
29.5 / 7.1 = 4.154929577464789 remainder 1.1000000000000014
```

Look at the accuracy! Java treats decimal values as doubles (accurate to 15 digits), unless you tell it otherwise.

Now let's try assigning expressions to variables. We'll start with some simple **ints**.

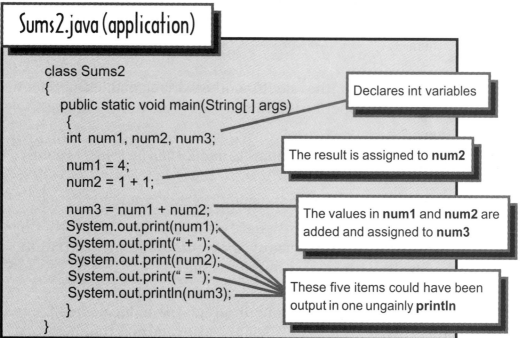

Sums2.java (application)

```
class Sums2
{
    public static void main(String[ ] args)
    {
    int  num1, num2, num3;

    num1 = 4;
    num2 = 1 + 1;

    num3 = num1 + num2;
    System.out.print(num1);
    System.out.print(" + ");
    System.out.print(num2);
    System.out.print(" = ");
    System.out.println(num3);
    }
}
```

Declares int variables

The result is assigned to **num2**

The values in **num1** and **num2** are added and assigned to **num3**

These five items could have been output in one ungainly **println**

This should give a single line output:

    4 + 2 = 6

Use the program as a basis for exploring.

- Try different values – see what happens when the total exceds 2,147,483,647 (the upper limit of the **int**'s range).

- Try with the other number types – **byte**, **short**, **long**, **float** and **double** (using decimal values with the last two).

- Try it with the other arithmetic operators – * / and %.

Increment and decrement

The ++ (increment) and –– (decrement) operators can be used to increase or decrease the value of a variable by 1.

    num++;

is quicker to type but has the same effect as:

    num = num + 1;

The operators can be used either prefix or postfix – i.e. written before or after the variable. If all you are doing is changing the value of that variable, it doesn't matter which form you use. These are identical:

    num++;
    ++num;

If you are assigning the value to another variable at the same time, the position of the operator is crucial.

    num2 = num1++;

assigns the inital value of **num1** to **num2**, then increments **num1**.

    num2 = ++num1;

increments **num1** before assigning its value to **num2**.

You can see this at work in the next example program. The other thing to watch for here is the use of *comments*. Anything written after a double slash // is ignored by the compiler.

    num1++;   // num now holds 6

Use comments freely in your programs to remind yourself (or tell others) what variables are being used for and how routines work.

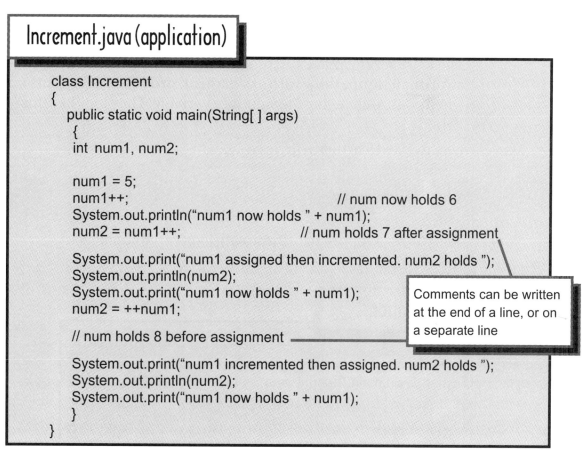

Increment.java (application)

```java
class Increment
{
    public static void main(String[ ] args)
    {
    int  num1, num2;

    num1 = 5;
    num1++;                                    // num now holds 6
    System.out.println("num1 now holds " + num1);
    num2 = num1++;                   // num holds 7 after assignment

    System.out.print("num1 assigned then incremented. num2 holds ");
    System.out.println(num2);
    System.out.print("num1 now holds " + num1);
    num2 = ++num1;

    // num holds 8 before assignment

    System.out.print("num1 incremented then assigned. num2 holds ");
    System.out.println(num2);
    System.out.print("num1 now holds " + num1);
    }
}
```

Comments can be written at the end of a line, or on a separate line

This program outputs:

```
num1 now holds 6
num1 assigned then incremented. num2 holds 6
num1 now holds 7
num1 incremented then assigned. num2 holds 8
num1 now holds 8
```

Common errors: No 2

The longer the program and the bigger the gap between declaring a variable and using it, the more likely you are to spell it wrong (or use the wrong mix of capitals and lower case letters).

Keep names simple, keep them meaningful, and be consistent in your use of capitals.

Assignment operators

These are very neat, as any C programmer will tell you. They combine an arithmetic operator with assignment, producing shortcuts for when you are changing the value of a variable. They look like this:

    += –= *= /=   %=

and are used like this:

    num += 2;

which is the same as:

    num = num + 2;

You will really appreciate these with long variable names!

Here are some assignment operators at work.

AssOp.java (application)

```java
class AssOp
{
    public static void main(String[ ] args)
    {
    int  num;

System.out.println("Think of a number");
    num = 7;
System.out.println("Double it");
    num *= 2;
System.out.println("Add 6");
    num += 6;
    System.out.println("Divide by 2");
    num /= 2;
    System.out.println("Take away the number you first thought of");
    num -= 7;
    System.out.println("The answer is 3");
    System.out.println("Calculation gives " + num);
    }
}
```

Operator precedence

The calculations so far have been simple ones, with only one operator. You can have Java expressions with several operators and values – just as you can on paper. The rules of precedence apply here, much as in ordinary arithmetic.

Where an expression has several operators, multiplication and division are done first, then addition and subtraction, and finally the assignment operators (though these are normally used only in simple calculations). If part of the expression is enclosed in brackets, that part is evaluated before the rest. e.g.:

    2 + 3 * 4 – (9 - 3) / 2

has its bracketed operation dealt with:

    2 + 3 * 4 – 6 / 2

then its multiplication and division:

    2 + 12 - 3

and finally the addition and subtraction:

    11

Where you have a sequence of multiplication and division (or addition and subtraction), it does not matter which you do first. e.g.:

    4 * 6 / 3   =   24 / 3   =   8
    or   =   4 * 2   =   8

Take note

Java also has *bitwise* operators that can change the values of individual bits within a byte. They are mainly used for manipulating memory and input/output streams, and are beyond the scope of a Made Simple book.

Arrays

Arrays let you store and manipulate information in bulk. Use them wherever you have a lot of data of the same type – list of names, sets of co-ordinates, results from surveys and the like.

The basic principles behind arrays are simple. Instead of having 10, 100 or 1 million or more variables each with a unique name, you have one name which refers to the whole set, with each individual *element* identified by its *subscript* – its position in the set. The subscript is written in [square brackets] after the array name.

As the subscript can be a variable, you have a simple way of accessing any – or all – the elements in the array. We will look at this properly in the next chapter when we get on to ways of repeating actions, but here's a simple example to show what is possible. Suppose you had an array of 1,000 numbers (**num**) and a variable (**count**). If you ran **count** through the full range of subscripts, while repeating this single line:

```
System.out.println( num[count]);
```

it would display all the numbers in the array. If those numbers had been stored in individual variables, you would have needed 1,000 **println**s to display them!

Initialising arrays

It takes a little more work to set up an array than it does to set up a primitive variable, such as an **int** or **char**. The system needs to know what type of data is to be stored, and how many elements there will be. A typical declaration statement looks like this:

```
int[] number = new int[100];
```

This sets up an **int** array, called **number**. The **new** constructor (the method that creates objects) allocates memory space for 100 **int**s. Numbering always starts from 0, so the subscripts for the elements in this array will run from 0 to 99. Notice the square [brackets] again.

An array element can be used wherever you would use a simple variable of the same type. You can see this in the following program – the only real difference in the assignment and println statements is the presence of the subscript in the variable name.

Arrays.java (application)

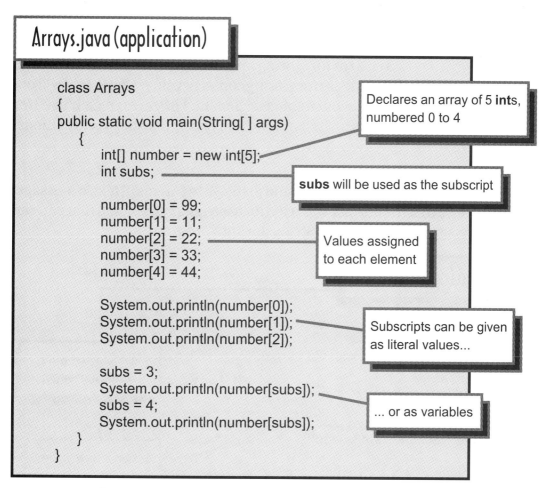

```
class Arrays
{
public static void main(String[ ] args)
    {
        int[] number = new int[5];
        int subs;

        number[0] = 99;
        number[1] = 11;
        number[2] = 22;
        number[3] = 33;
        number[4] = 44;

        System.out.println(number[0]);
        System.out.println(number[1]);
        System.out.println(number[2]);

        subs = 3;
        System.out.println(number[subs]);
        subs = 4;
        System.out.println(number[subs]);
    }
}
```

Declares an array of 5 **int**s, numbered 0 to 4

subs will be used as the subscript

Values assigned to each element

Subscripts can be given as literal values...

... or as variables

Save the code as 'Arrays.java', compile it and run it, and you should see something like this:

Take note

You can do a lot more with arrays when you use loops — see the next Chapter.

49

String objects

Java has two classes for storing text. **String** is the simpler structure. Objects of this type are for storing constant values – ones that will not be changed, except by simple assignment. They are typically used for holding messages to the user, and for passing data between methods.

Using Strings

This trivial example stores and displays two items of text in message. Note that the normal '=' is used for assigning values, and that you can assign a new value to a String during a program.

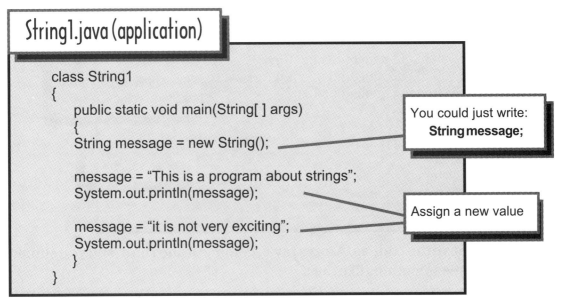

```
String1.java (application)

class String1
{
    public static void main(String[ ] args)
    {
    String message = new String();

    message = "This is a program about strings";
    System.out.println(message);

    message = "it is not very exciting";
    System.out.println(message);
    }
}
```

You could just write:
String message;

Assign a new value

String[ ] args

We have meet this often enough already – perhaps it's time to see what it does.

```
main(String [ ] args)
```

sets up an array of String – with an unspecified number of elements – called *args* (short for arguments). As you will see later (page 96), variables or classes given in brackets after a method's name, are there to collect *parameters* – data passed to methods. In this case, the *args[ ]* array will collect any text that is typed in the command line after the program name. When the program is executed, the system copies the first item into *args[0]*, the next into *args[1]*, and so on. Practical uses for this technique include giving filenames to a program for processing, and providing test data for a program.

The example below copies the args[ ] values into the Strings, firstName and surName, then greets the user.

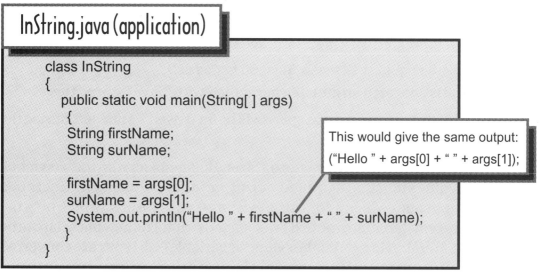

InString.java (application)

```
class InString
{
    public static void main(String[ ] args)
    {
    String firstName;
    String surName;

    firstName = args[0];
    surName = args[1];
    System.out.println("Hello " + firstName + " " + surName);
    }
}
```

This would give the same output:
("Hello " + args[0] + " " + args[1]);

Compile the program, and when you run it, type your first name and surname at the end of the command line. You must give this program at least two names – it will crash if it tries to copy an *args[ ]* string that is not there, though it will ignore any extra ones.

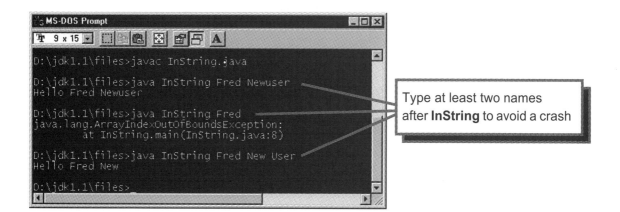

```
MS-DOS Prompt
T  9 x 15

D:\jdk1.1\files>javac InString.java

D:\jdk1.1\files>java InString Fred Newuser
Hello Fred Newuser

D:\jdk1.1\files>java InString Fred
java.lang.ArrayIndexOutOfBoundsException:
        at InString.main(InString.java:8)

D:\jdk1.1\files>java InString Fred New User
Hello Fred New

D:\jdk1.1\files>
```

Type at least two names after **InString** to avoid a crash

StringBuffers

StringBuffer objects are more flexible than simple Strings. The data held in these can be manipulated by the program. If you want to edit, add to or otherwise work on text, store it in a StringBuffer.

StringBuffer objects can be created in three ways:

StringBuffer s1 = new StringBuffer();

This creates *s1* and allocates space for the default 16 characters.

StringBuffer s2 = new StringBuffer(40);

s2 is created with initial storage space of 40 characters.

StringBuffer s3 = new StringBuffer("Java ");

s3 is allocated an initial 4 characters, with "Java" stored there.

In all cases, the storage space will be increased, as needed, during the program's execution.

You cannot assign a value to a StringBuffer object with the '=' symbol. Values must be assigned during creation, or using the methods append(), which adds to the existing text, or insert() which puts the new material into the text at a selected point. The new material can be a literal string or number value or variable – all types are converted into characters for inclusion. The next program demonstrates this.

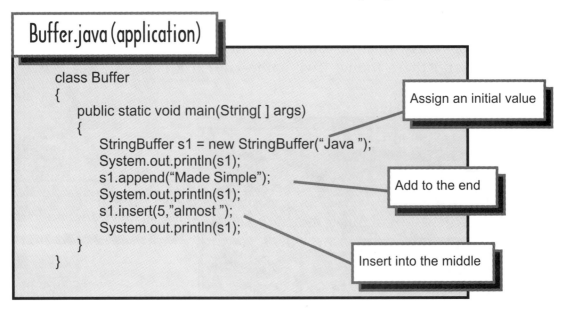

Buffer.java (application)

```
class Buffer
{
    public static void main(String[ ] args)
    {
        StringBuffer s1 = new StringBuffer("Java ");
        System.out.println(s1);
        s1.append("Made Simple");
        System.out.println(s1);
        s1.insert(5,"almost ");
        System.out.println(s1);
    }
}
```

Assign an initial value

Add to the end

Insert into the middle

The output from this program is:

```
Java
Java Made Simple
Java almost Made Simple
```

Text from the keyboard

On page 40, you saw that it was possible, though not simple, to read characters from the keyboard. If we want a string of text, we can use the same technique, and append the characters into a StringBuffer. Here's a program that will do the job – the **do ... while** loop that keeps it all going is explained in the next chapter (page 65).

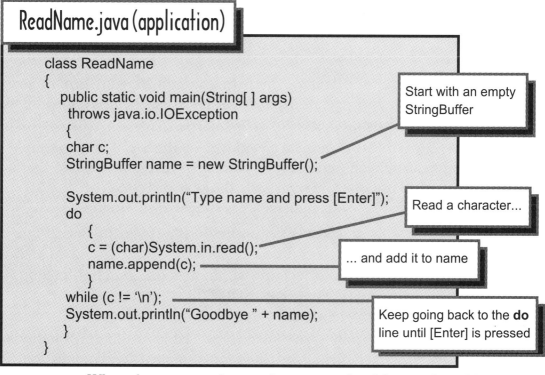

ReadName.java (application)

```java
class ReadName
{
    public static void main(String[ ] args)
     throws java.io.IOException
     {
     char c;
     StringBuffer name = new StringBuffer();

     System.out.println("Type name and press [Enter]");
     do
        {
        c = (char)System.in.read();
        name.append(c);
        }
     while (c != '\n');
     System.out.println("Goodbye " + name);
     }
}
```

Start with an empty StringBuffer

Read a character...

... and add it to name

Keep going back to the **do** line until [Enter] is pressed

When the program is run, the screen should something like this:

```
Type name and press [Enter]
Fred NewUser
Goodbye Fred NewUser
```

The scope of variables

The shape of Java programs

So far, the example programs have had a very simple structure – a set of statements inside the **main()** method. In practice, most programs will contain several methods, each performing a specific function, and all controlled and run from **main()**. As you will see later, applets normally have at least two, and usually far more, methods.

This approach makes programming easier in any language – small blocks of code are simpler to develop and test, as there is less to go wrong – and you can sometimes reuse a method in a new program, and save some effort! Methods are integral to Object Oriented programming – when working with classes, you often have to write methods to extend or replace existing methods in the classes that you are using.

Scope

Variables can be declared more or less anywhere in a program – as long as they are declared before you try to use them! Where they are declared affects where they can be used.

- Variables declared at class level – at the top of the program – can be accessed from any point in the program. These declarations must start with the keyword static, which allocates permanent memory space to the variable.
- Variables declared within a method can only be used within that method.
- Variables can be declared within structures such as **for** loops (see page 60). They only exist within the loop and are discarded when the program exits from the loop.
- The same name can be used for variables in different methods, without confusing the program – though it may confuse you!

ProgShape.java shows the structure of a program with two methods. It also illustrates the scope of variables. **b**, a class level variable, can be accessed from both methods. There are two variables called **a** which have different values in the two methods.

ProgShape.java (application)

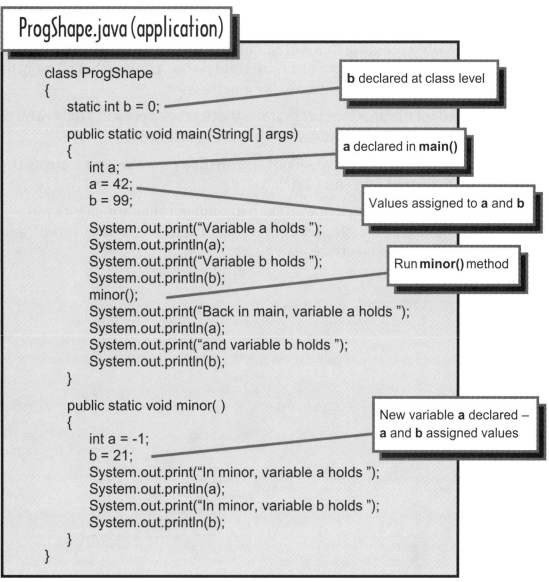

```
class ProgShape
{
    static int b = 0;              ──── b declared at class level

    public static void main(String[ ] args)
    {                              ──── a declared in main()
        int a;
        a = 42;                    ──── Values assigned to a and b
        b = 99;

        System.out.print("Variable a holds ");
        System.out.println(a);
        System.out.print("Variable b holds ");
        System.out.println(b);
        minor();                   ──── Run minor() method
        System.out.print("Back in main, variable a holds ");
        System.out.println(a);
        System.out.print("and variable b holds ");
        System.out.println(b);
    }

    public static void minor( )
    {                              ──── New variable a declared –
        int a = -1;                     a and b assigned values
        b = 21;
        System.out.print("In minor, variable a holds ");
        System.out.println(a);
        System.out.print("In minor, variable b holds ");
        System.out.println(b);
    }
}
```

The output from this program is shown below.

```
Variable a holds 42
Variable b holds 99
In minor, variable a holds -1
In minor, variable b holds 21
Back in main, variable a holds 42
and variable b holds 21
```

Exercises

1 Write a program that will calculate a person's age in days, working from their age in days, months and years. Assume that all months have 30 days – it will make life much easier!

2 Adapt the previous program so that it takes a person's date of birth and today's date, and works out the age from that.

   Hint: You should work out the birthday and today's date as the number of days since 1900.

3 Write a program that will take two command line arguments and add them to a StringBuffer containing the phrase "You entered" and output the new string.

3 Program flow

Testing values

Program flow refers to the order in which a program's instructions are carried out. So far, all the example programs have run straight through a sequence, then stopped. There are few practical uses for such simple programs. The addition of loops and branches makes programs far more useful and powerful. In a loop, a set of instructions will be repeated a fixed number of times, or until a condition is met. Branches take the flow off down different routes, depending upon the values held by variables. Before we go any further, let's see how we can test values.

Relational operators

These are used to compare variables with values or with the contents of other variables. There are six relational operators:

```
==  equal to        <  less than       <=  less than or equal to
!=  not equal to     >  greater than    >=  greater than or equal to
```

Notice that the equality test uses a double equals sign '=='. The single sign '=' is used for assigning values. Typical test expressions are:

```
(x < 99)
(newNum != oldNum)
```

Tests are enclosed in brackets, and return a Boolean value – **true** or **false**. You don't normally need to worry about this – just use the test – but occasionally it is useful to store the result of the test in a variable, for reference later in the program, e.g.

```
boolean    result;                    // create a boolean variable
...
result = (newNum > oldNum)            // store the test result
...
if (result == true)                   // same as if (newNum > oldNum)
```

Logical operators

The relational operators test variables against one value at a time, but you often want to check if a variable falls into a range of values, or is one of several possibilities. This is where the *logical operators* come into play.

AND and OR

The **&&** (AND) operator compares the results from two tests, with the expression being true if both tests are true.

    ((x >= 20) && (x <= 30))

This expression is true for all values of **x** from 20 to 30.

With an | | (OR) operator, the expression is true if either or both of the tests are true.

    ((x > 100) || (y > 200))

This expression is true if **x** is greater than 100 or **y** is greater than 200, or if both are over their limits.

A logical expression can have more than two tests and can include both **&&** and | |. In mixed expressions, **&&** is evaluated first, unless you use brackets – here, as in arithmetic, anything in brackets is evaluated first.

    ((x >= 20) && (x <= 30) || (y > 200))

For this to be true, the **x** value must be between 20 and 30, or the **y** value over 200 – in which case, the **x** value is irrelevant.

    (((x > 100) || (y > 200)) && (edgecheck = true))

This is true if either, or both, the **x** and **y** values are over the limit, and **edgecheck** has been set to true.

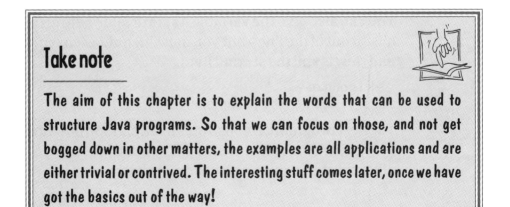

Take note

The aim of this chapter is to explain the words that can be used to structure Java programs. So that we can focus on those, and not get bogged down in other matters, the examples are all applications and are either trivial or contrived. The interesting stuff comes later, once we have got the basics out of the way!

for loops

The **for** loop allows you to repeat a set of instructions for a given number of times. The basic shape of the loop is:

```
for (var = start_value; end_test; change)
    { statement(s); }
```

When the program hits this line for the first time, the *var* is assigned its *start_value*. The following *statement*, or block of statements, are executed, and the flow loops back to the **for** line. The value of *var* is then adjusted as specified by the *change*. The *end_test* is performed – this typically compares the var with a given value, e.g. **counter < 100**. If the end value has not been reached, the statements are performed again, and flow continues to loop back until the *end_test* is met.

This simple **for** line:

```
for (counter = 0; counter <10 ; counter++)
```

sets up a loop that will repeat its statements a total of 10 times, as *counter* is incremented through the values 0 to 9.

The change does not have to be an increment. This loop will repeat 20 times, as counter is taken through the values 100, 95, 90, down to 0.

```
for (counter = 100; counter >0 ; counter = counter - 5)
```

If you like, the **for** variable can be declared within the statement. This would restrict its scope purely to the loop, and it would be discarded on exit from the loop.

```
for (int counter = 0; counter <10 ; counter++)
```

You can also give the variable its start value before the **for** line, and miss it out of the line – but you must include a semicolon, so that the *end_test* is still the second item.

```
int counter = 0
for ( ; counter <10 ; counter++)
```

The next program demonstrates a simple loop in action, producing a very basic times table display. Type it in and try it, then try it with different start values, end tests and changes.

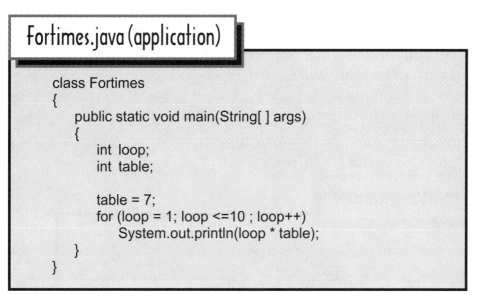

```
class Fortimes
{
    public static void main(String[ ] args)
    {
        int  loop;
        int  table;

        table = 7;
        for (loop = 1; loop <=10 ; loop++)
            System.out.println(loop * table);
    }
}
```

When compiled and run, it should display the numbers 7 to 70, in steps of 7.

Blocks of code

If you want to loop through a set of instructions, rather than a single statement, enclose the statements in curly {brackets}. For example, we can extend the program to display the loop counter as well as the multiple.

```
...
for (loop = 1; loop <=10 ; loop++)
    {
    System.out.print(loop);
    System.out.print(" x 7 = ");
    System.out.println(loop * table);
    }
...
```

The display is now:

        1 x 7 = 7
        2 x 7 = 14
        ...

Take note

You should use curly {brackets} in any situation where you need to keep lines of code together, not just in **for** loops.

Varying loop values

The number of times that a for loop is iterated (repeated) is determined by the start and end values, but these do not have to be fixed at design time. If either or both values are held in variables, they can be assigned by the program's user or calculated during its run.

In the next example, the end value is a random number – see the Detour, opposite, for an explanation of that line.

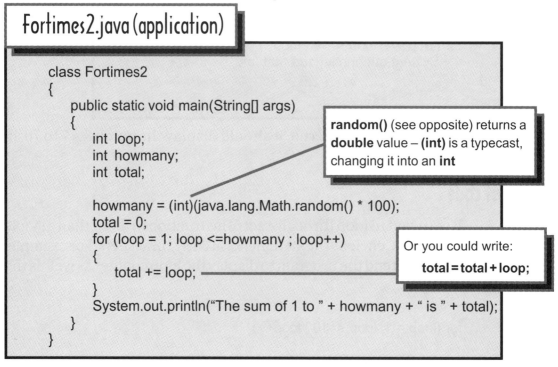

Fortimes2.java (application)

```
class Fortimes2
{
    public static void main(String[] args)
    {
        int  loop;
        int  howmany;
        int  total;

        howmany = (int)(java.lang.Math.random() * 100);
        total = 0;
        for (loop = 1; loop <=howmany ; loop++)
        {
            total += loop;
        }
        System.out.println("The sum of 1 to " + howmany + " is " + total);
    }
}
```

random() (see opposite) returns a **double** value – **(int)** is a typecast, changing it into an **int**

Or you could write:
total = total + loop;

Nested loops

Loops can be 'nested' inside one another, with the inner loop running its full course each time the program flow passes through the outer loop. It's a technique that you might use to read and array, or create a table of two (or more) dimensions.

The Nesting example creates a times table for the numbers 1 to 6, multiplying each in turn by 1 to 10. When you think that each of the loops could have a far higher end value, you realise just how much work you can get out of two or three lines of code, thanks to loops!

```
class Nesting
{
   public static void main(String[ ] args)
   {
   int  outer;
   int  inner;

   for (outer = 1; outer <= 6; outer++)
      {
      for (inner = 1; inner <= 10; inner++)
         System.out.print((inner * outer) + "\t");
      System.out.println();
      }
   }
}
```

Your output should look like this:

1	2	3	4	5	6	7	8	9	10
2	4	6	8	10	12	14	16	18	20
3	6	9	12	15	18	21	24	27	30
4	8	12	16	20	24	28	32	36	40
5	10	15	20	25	30	35	40	45	50
6	12	18	24	30	36	42	48	54	60

Detour: Random numbers

In the **java.lang.Math class** is a method, **random()**, which generates a random number in the range 0.0 to 1.0. Used at its simplest, e.g.

```
x = java.lang.Math.random();
```

will give you a fractional value less than 1. If you want a decent sized number, this must be mutiplied up. Multiply by 10 and the number will be in the range of 0 to 10 – but it will still be a fractional (double) value. If you want an integer, you must convert the expression by putting **(int)** at the start.

```
randNum = (int)(java.lang.Math.random() * 1000);
```

randNum will be a whole number between 0 and 999.

while loops

for loops are normally repeated for a set number of times. **while** loops give you greater flexibility in two ways:

- the exit test can check any variable, not just a loop counter;
- the exit test can be at the start or end of the loop – so, if the right condition is met, the loop's statement may not be performed at all.

The **while** loop takes this shape:

```
while (test)
{ statement(s); }
```

The system performs the test on entry to the loop, and before each repetition. Here's a very simple example, using a counter to determine the number of repetitions.

WhileEx.java (application)

```
class WhileEx
{
    public static void main(String[ ] args)
    {
    int  count = 0;
    while (count < 10)
        {
        count++;
        System.out.println(count);
        }
    }
}
```

One of the things to notice here is that this displays 1 to 10, even though the text is **count < 10**. That's because the increment and print is done after the test. Compare this with the equivalent for loop, and keep the difference in mind when setting up loop tests.

```
for (count = 0;count < 10; count++)
    {
        System.out.println(count);        //displays 0 to 9
    }
```

do ...while

This variation moves the test to the end of the loop. The statements within it are therefore always performed at least once. Its shape is:

```
do
    { statement(s); }
while (test);
```

Notice that there is a semi-colon at the end of the **while** line – this is essential.

The following program demonstrates the do ... while loop, and again uses the random() method to emphasise that the repetition can be controlled by values arising from within the loop.

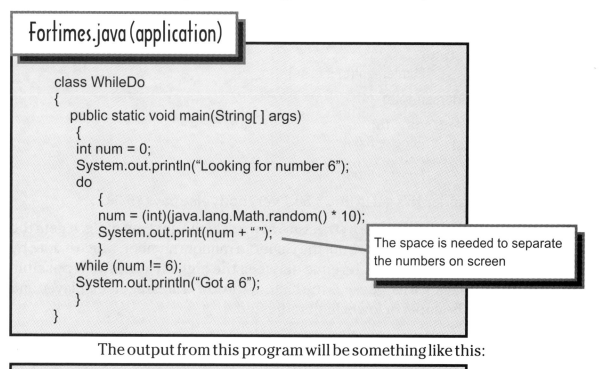

Fortimes.java (application)

```
class WhileDo
{
    public static void main(String[ ] args)
    {
        int num = 0;
        System.out.println("Looking for number 6");
        do
            {
            num = (int)(java.lang.Math.random() * 10);
            System.out.print(num + " ");
            }
        while (num != 6);
        System.out.println("Got a 6");
    }
}
```

The space is needed to separate the numbers on screen

The output from this program will be something like this:

```
Looking for number 6
4 9 1 3 5 0 4 3 4 4 3 9 1 6  Got a 6
```

Branching with if

Loops make programs powerful, giving them the ability to process masses of data. Branches make them flexible, allowing them to vary their actions in response to incoming data. The simplest form of branch uses the **if** keyword. This is the basic syntax:

```
if (test)
    { statement(s) if true}
```

The test checks the value held by a variable. **if** the test proves true, the program performs the statement(s), otherwise they are ignored.

A variation on this uses the **else** keyword, which handles the actions to perform if the test does not proves true. The syntax is:

```
if (test)
    { statement(s) if true}
else
    { statement(s) if false}
```

For example:

```
if (age < 18)
    { cost = 3.50}
else
    { cost = 5.00}
```

Under 18's get in for £3.50. Everybody else pays £5.00.

You can see the **if** structure at work in the next example. It gets the computer to work out the value of a random number, which it does by splitting the difference between the highest and lowest possible values. If its 'guess' is too high, or too low, a message is displayed and the upper or lower limits adjusted.

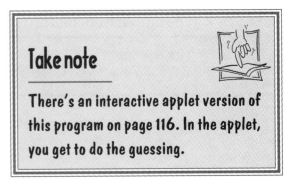

Take note

There's an interactive applet version of this program on page 116. In the applet, you get to do the guessing.

Guess1.java (application)

```
class Guess1

{
  public static void main(String[ ] args)
  {
    int  target = (int)(java.lang.Math.random() * 100);
    int  guess;
    int  count = 0;
    int  lower = 0;
    int  upper = 100;
    do
    {
      count ++;
      guess = (upper - lower)/2 + lower;
      if (guess > target)
      {
        upper = guess;
        System.out.println("Too high - trying again" + guess);
      }
      if (guess < target)
      {
        lower = guess;
        System.out.println("Too low - trying again" + guess);
      }
    }
    while(guess != target);
    System.out.println("Got it in " + count + " goes");
  }
}
```

> Results in a number half way between the upper and lower limits

> This could have been done as a while loop, but we would then have had to assign an initial value to guess.

A typical output is shown below – the computer never takes more than seven goes. Why not?

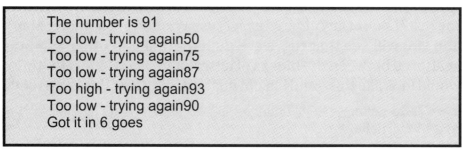

```
The number is 91
Too low - trying again50
Too low - trying again75
Too low - trying again87
Too high - trying again93
Too low - trying again90
Got it in 6 goes
```

Multiple branching

The basic **if** structure has the beauty of simplicity – it shows very clearly the relationship between the test and the outcome. However, it is not always the best solution. Consider this problem. You want to analyse incoming characters to see if they are upper or lower case letters, digits, spaces or symbols. Here's the first draft of a program that should do the job.

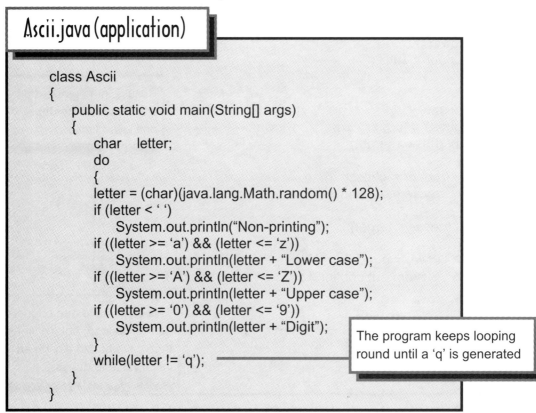

Ascii.java (application)

```
class Ascii
{
    public static void main(String[] args)
    {
        char    letter;
        do
        {
        letter = (char)(java.lang.Math.random() * 128);
        if (letter < ' ')
            System.out.println("Non-printing");
        if ((letter >= 'a') && (letter <= 'z'))
            System.out.println(letter + "Lower case");
        if ((letter >= 'A') && (letter <= 'Z'))
            System.out.println(letter + "Upper case");
        if ((letter >= '0') && (letter <= '9'))
            System.out.println(letter + "Digit");
        }
        while(letter != 'q');
    }
}
```

The program keeps looping round until a 'q' is generated

So far, so good. This handles the non-printing characters (0 to 31) up to space, and the sets, 'a' to 'z', 'A' to 'Z' and '0' to '9'. Now what about the rest? Look at any character set (use Windows' Character Map), and you will see that there are punctuation and other symbols scattered between the blocks of letters and digits. A test for these would look like this – and I'm not guaranteeing that this is correct!:

```
if ((letter >= ' ') && (letter <= '0') || (letter >= '9') && (letter <= 'a') || (letter >= '\')
&& (letter <= 'A') || (letter >= 'Z'))
```

68

Here's a better solution. The **if ... else** structure gives two branches from the same test – one to follow if it is true, and one if it is false. This can be extended to handle multiple branching.

```
if (test1)
    {statement(s) if test1 is true}
else if (test2)
    {statement(s) if test2 is true}

...
else
    {statement(s) if no tests are true}
```

If test1 is false, the program tries test2, and failing that, tries the next. If all the tests prove false, the program performs the statements after the final **else**. Here's a better solution to the character analysis problem.

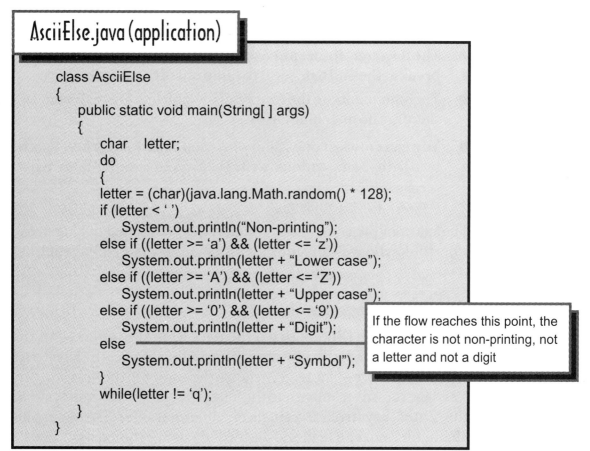

AsciiElse.java (application)

```java
class AsciiElse
{
    public static void main(String[ ] args)
    {
        char    letter;
        do
        {
        letter = (char)(java.lang.Math.random() * 128);
        if (letter < ' ')
            System.out.println("Non-printing");
        else if ((letter >= 'a') && (letter <= 'z'))
            System.out.println(letter + "Lower case");
        else if ((letter >= 'A') && (letter <= 'Z'))
            System.out.println(letter + "Upper case");
        else if ((letter >= '0') && (letter <= '9'))
            System.out.println(letter + "Digit");
        else
            System.out.println(letter + "Symbol");
        }
        while(letter != 'q');
    }
}
```

If the flow reaches this point, the character is not non-printing, not a letter and not a digit

Switch

The **switch** structure can be used to replace a whole set of **if** statements, where these all test the same simple variable for different values. A typical use would be with a menu, where the switch directs the flow to the chosen option's routine. The basic shape of the structure is:

```
switch (var)
    {
    case value1 : statement(s); break;
    case value2 : statement(s); break;
    ...
    default :  statement(s); break;
    }
```

● The *var* being tested will typically be an int or char.

● The *values* must be literal values – not other variables.

● The switch does a simple match, comparing each of the *values* with the *var* – you cannot use the relational operators here.

● The flow runs from one case line to the next, unless you put a **break** at the end to force it to jump out of the switch block.

● The statements on the (optional) **default** line are performed if there are no matching cases.

● You can only test one value with each **case**. If several values to lead to the same actions, write them on successive lines. e.g.:

```
case 'q' :;
case 'Q' : {exit routine}...
```

The following program shows **switch** at work. The choice value is read from the keyboard – and look for a moment at that reading routine.

```
choice = (char)System.in.read();
excess = (char)System.in.read();
excess = (char)System.in.read();
```

You must press [Enter] to get the data from the buffer – but the [Enter] keystroke is itself stored in the buffer. In a PC, the keystroke is two characters – 'line feed', to move the cursor to the next line, and 'carriage return', to move it to the left of the screen. In some systems the [Enter] keystroke is a single newline character. These surplus characters must be read and discarded – hence the *excess*... lines.

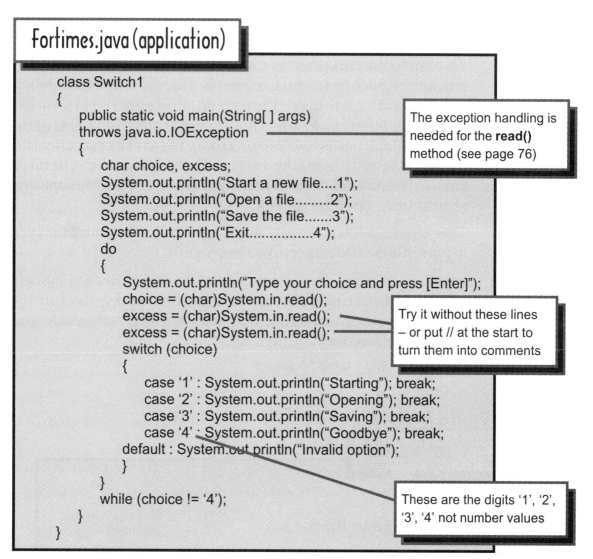

Fortimes.java (application)

```
class Switch1
{
    public static void main(String[ ] args)
    throws java.io.IOException
    {
        char choice, excess;
        System.out.println("Start a new file....1");
        System.out.println("Open a file.........2");
        System.out.println("Save the file.......3");
        System.out.println("Exit...............4");
        do
        {
            System.out.println("Type your choice and press [Enter]");
            choice = (char)System.in.read();
            excess = (char)System.in.read();
            excess = (char)System.in.read();
            switch (choice)
            {
                case '1' : System.out.println("Starting"); break;
                case '2' : System.out.println("Opening"); break;
                case '3' : System.out.println("Saving"); break;
                case '4' : System.out.println("Goodbye"); break;
                default : System.out.println("Invalid option");
            }
        }
        while (choice != '4');
    }
}
```

The exception handling is needed for the **read()** method (see page 76)

Try it without these lines – or put // at the start to turn them into comments

These are the digits '1', '2', '3', '4' not number values

Here's a typical output:

```
Start a new file....1
Open a file.........2
Save the file........3
Exit.....................4
Type your choice and press [Enter]
2
Opening
Type your choice and press [Enter]
4
Goodbye
```

Using methods

You can write a program as a single block of code, but beyond a certain size, such programs become hard to read and hard to debug. A better solution is to divide the code up into distinct blocks, each of which is defined as a new method. **main()** *calls* (transfers to) the method when it needs to execute its code, and after its execution, the flow returns from the method to **main()**. This process can be taken further, with one new method calling another. Program flow always returns to the line after the call.

The example below is actually very short, but I'm not going to ask you to type in lots of lines just to prove a point!

First, here's the program as one block of code. It raises a number to an integer power, using a loop. To see how it works, 'dry run' the program on paper, writing down the values held by *temp* and *loop* as the program runs through the loop:

loop	temp	temp * number
1	1	4
2	4	16
3	16	64

Power.java (application)

```
class Power
{
    public static void main(String[ ] args)
    {
        int  number = 4;
        int  p = 3;
        int temp = 1;
        int loop;

        for (loop = 1; loop <= p; loop++)
            temp = temp * number;
        System.out.println(number + " to the power of " + p + " = " + temp);
    }
}
```

Use any values you like, changing the type to **long** if very large

Now let's see how this looks using a method. In this first version, the calculation and the output line are all transferred to the new **powerOf()** method.

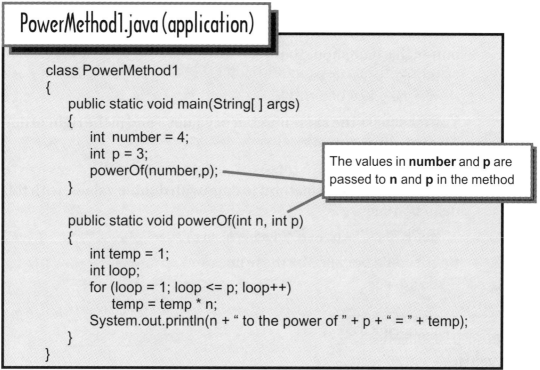

PowerMethod1.java (application)

```
class PowerMethod1
{
    public static void main(String[ ] args)
    {
        int  number = 4;
        int  p = 3;
        powerOf(number,p);
    }

    public static void powerOf(int n, int p)
    {
        int temp = 1;
        int loop;
        for (loop = 1; loop <= p; loop++)
            temp = temp * n;
        System.out.println(n + " to the power of " + p + " = " + temp);
    }
}
```

The values in **number** and **p** are passed to **n** and **p** in the method

Notice its definition line:

    public static void powerOf(int n, int p)

The parameters **(int n, int p)** take two integer values from the calling line, and they act as normal variables within **powerOf()**. **number** in **main()** is passed to **n** in **powerOf()**, and **p** in **main()** is passed to **p** in **powerOf()**.

The choice of names is deliberate – the names of parameters can be the same as or different from those of the variables that are passed to them. The parameters and variables in powerOf() are completely separate from those in main(). p in main() and p in powerOf() are two different items, and neither can be used from the other method.

Parameters

When passing values to a method, you must pass the right type of data, though it can be either as a variable or a literal value. This call to power() would also work:

```
powerOf(5,5);
```

Add that line to **main()**, compile and run the program again. The output this time should be:

```
4 to the power of 3 = 64
5 to the power of 5 = 3125
```

You must pass the same number of values – and in the right order. This would not compile:

```
powerOf(5);
```

if we had written the method to cope with double values, with this definition line:

```
public static int powerOf(double n, int p)
```

then it could be called by these lines:

```
double num;
...
powerOf(num, p)
powerOf(5.234, 3)
```

Return values

Let's turn our attention to the start of the definition line.

```
public static void...
```

- **public** says that the method can be accessed by other methods.

- **static** allocates permanent memory space for its variables.

- **void** refers to the value returned by the method.

void methods return nothing, but methods can return values of any type. If you have used other programming languages, void methods act as subroutines, while those returning values act as functions.

Here's the Power program again, this time rewritten so that the **powerOf()** method returns an **int** value.

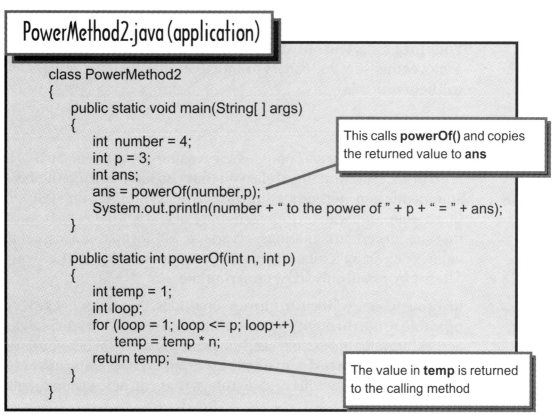

PowerMethod2.java (application)

```
class PowerMethod2
{
    public static void main(String[ ] args)
    {
        int  number = 4;
        int  p = 3;
        int ans;
        ans = powerOf(number,p);
        System.out.println(number + " to the power of " + p + " = " + ans);
    }

    public static int powerOf(int n, int p)
    {
        int temp = 1;
        int loop;
        for (loop = 1; loop <= p; loop++)
            temp = temp * n;
        return temp;
    }
}
```

This calls **powerOf()** and copies the returned value to **ans**

The value in **temp** is returned to the calling method

This time the definition line reads:

```
public static int powerOf(int n, int p)
```

This creates a method that returns an int value – and the line that does this is at the end:

```
return temp;
```

Notice the calling line in main().

```
ans = powerOf(number,p);
```

A method that returns a value must be treated as a value. You cannot call it with a simple statement:

```
powerOf(number,p);
```

This would work for a void method, but if a value is returned it must be assigned to a variable, printed or otherwise used as a value. This would work:

```
System.out.println( "The answer is " + powerOf(number,p));
```

Errors and exceptions

Your programs will not always be perfect – no programmer ever achieves this – but you can try to anticipate possible errors, and Java will help with this.

Runtime errors

The fact that a program compiles successfully does not mean that it is error-free. Compilation tells you that you have written the Java statements and methods using the correct syntax. It won't tell you that a **while** loop will run forever as the exit test will never be true, or that – under certain conditions – a variable will not hold an acceptable value, or an array's subscript will be outside the range of the array. These errors will only show up at runtime.

Rigorous testing will help to turn up some bugs. You must check every possible route through your program, and test all variables right across the range of possible – and impossible – values. When you have done all you can to test it, hand the program to people who have not seen it before. They will try to do things that you never thought of!

If you cannot see where a program is going wrong, insert statements to display the values held in key variables or to mark the progress through a routine:

```
System.out.println("The total is now " + total);
System.out.println("Into the calculating loop");
```

These *stubs* (in the jargon) are best used one or two at a time to narrow the bug-search first to the method, then the line that is causing the trouble.

Exceptions

Runtime errors are probably less common in Java programs than those written in other languages because of its exception-handling. Those methods that are likely to hit errors – for example those that open files, which may not be present – *throw exceptions* (a kind of error report). When using these methods, you must add code to *catch* the exceptions.

For example, when you try to open a file, there is a real possibility that it may not be there. Use this line by itself...

```
FileInputStream inStream = new FileInputStream(inFile);
```

... and you will get an error message telling you that you must catch **FileNotFoundException** on the **new FileInputStream()** statement.

The solution is to enclose the statement in a **try** block. This is followed by one or more **catch** blocks. Each of these has at the start the name of the exception being caught.

```
try
{
    FileInputStream inStream = new FileInputStream(inFile);
}
catch (FileNotFoundException e)
{
    System.out.println("Error: " + e);
}
```

It is up to you what you do with the exception when you've caught it. Here the error message e is printed – this is useful for debugging and as feedback to the user. We could have asked the user for another filename and looped back to try again. **catch** blocks can even be left empty – but they must be there!

You will find some examples of exception handling in some of the programs in Chapters 7 and 8.

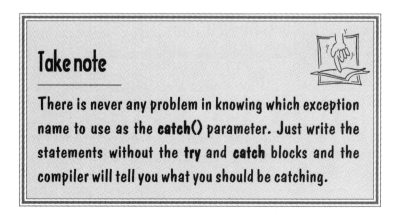

Take note

There is never any problem in knowing which exception name to use as the **catch()** parameter. Just write the statements without the **try** and **catch** blocks and the compiler will tell you what you should be catching.

Exercises

1   Write a program, using two loops, to produce this pattern of asterisks:

```
*
**
***
****
*****
******
*******
********
*********
**********
```

2   Find out how fast Java runs on your PC. Write a program that displays "Starting to count", runs through a loop, then displays "Done".

How long does it take your PC to count to 500,000? How long to count to 5,000,000?

3   How random are the numbers produced by **random()**? Set up an array of 10 **int**s, then generate random numbers in the range 0 to 9 and increment the matching element in the array. This should loop round for at least 1,000 times.

4   Write a program that takes a character and, using **if** tests and and a **switch** block, prints out a message to say whether it is upper case, lower case, digit, non-printing or a symbol. At least three symbols should be individually recognised.

4　Applet basics

The Applet methods

All applets are based on the Applet class, which contains a whole batch of ready-made methods. Some of these are run automatically in response to system activity. The first example in this chapter looks at these key methods:

init() is run when the applet is first loaded, and only then. If you have variables that need to be given initial values, this is where it should be done.

start() is run when the applet is loaded, and again whenever the applet's page is reloaded. If you want to restart an action when someone returns to a page, do it from this method.

stop() is run when the browser is shut down or another page is opened.

paint() redraws the display when the page is loaded or reloaded.

The definition of the Applet class includes these methods, but as blanks like this:

```
public void init()
{
}
```

They don't do anything, but by being there they link the method names to the relevant system events. If you write your own **init()** method, it will override the original, and be performed when the applet is first loaded.

In the next example applet, the **init()**, **start()** and **stop()** methods have each been given a line that assigns or adds more text to the StringBuffer object *message*. The **paint()** method then displays it. Don't worry about how the **drawString()** line works for the moment, we'll come to that shortly. The important thing here is what happens when you run the applet.

Type it in and compile it, and link it into an HTML file – the code for a suitable testing page is given opposite.

StartStop.java (applet)

```java
import java.awt.*;
import java.applet.*;

public class StartStop extends Applet
{
    StringBuffer message;
    public void init()
    {
        message = new StringBuffer("Init done ...");
    }
    public void start()
    {
        message.append("Started...");
    }
    public void stop()
    {
        message.append("Stopped...");
    }
    public void paint(Graphics g)
    {
        g.drawString(message.toString(), 150, 50);
    }
}
```

- Standard imports
- initial text of message
- added to message when applet starts
- added when applet stops

test.htm

```html
<HTML>
<HEAD>
  <TITLE> Applet tester </TITLE>
</HEAD>
<BODY>

<P>Applet output:</P>
<P><APPLET CODE="StartStop.class" WIDTH=500 HEIGHT=200>
</APPLET></P>

</BODY>
</HTML>
```

The AppletViewer

After you have compiled the applet, and written the HTML file, view it through the AppletViewer with the command:

    appletviewer test.htm

Pull down the **Applet** menu and give the commands **Stop**, then **Start**, several times. Your applet should now look like this.

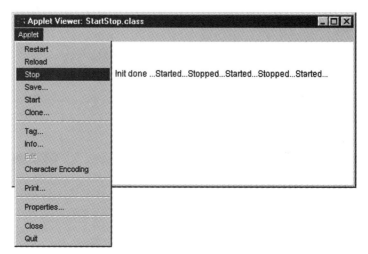

You should have noticed that a **Stop** clears the display, but when a **Start** is then given, and the display is restored, *message* has had "Stop... Start..." appended to it.

While you have the AppletViewer running, you might like to explore some of its other commands.

Restart   clears the display, resets any variables and runs **init()**.

Reload   in practice, normally the same as Restart.

Clone...   opens a new window and runs a copy of the applet there – use this to compare the applet at different stages of execution.

Tag...   shows the <APPLET...> tag that hosts the applet.

Print...   copies the display to your printer.

Close/Quit   Shuts down the applet and the viewer.

The other commands can be ignored for now.

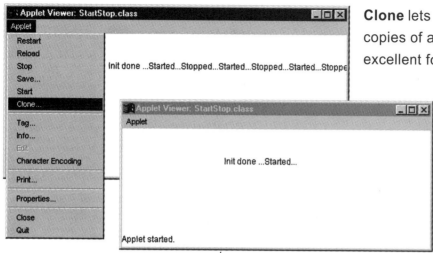

Clone lets you view multiple copies of an applet – excellent for testing!

Tag... displays the HTML tag that is running the applet

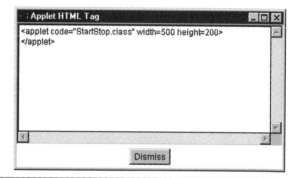

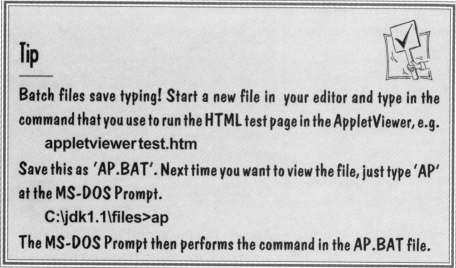

Tip

Batch files save typing! Start a new file in your editor and type in the command that you use to run the HTML test page in the AppletViewer, e.g.

    appletviewer test.htm

Save this as 'AP.BAT'. Next time you want to view the file, just type 'AP' at the MS-DOS Prompt.

    C:\jdk1.1\files>ap

The MS-DOS Prompt then performs the command in the AP.BAT file.

Applets in the browser

Applets automatically run the **start()** method when their host page is opened or re-opened, and run the **stop()** method when the browser moves off to another page. Set your browser off, and test this.

1 Load the test page into your browser, with the Open – File command. The message should show you that the **init()** and **start()** methods have been performed.display.

2 Now load another page in – any page will do. Click the browser's back button 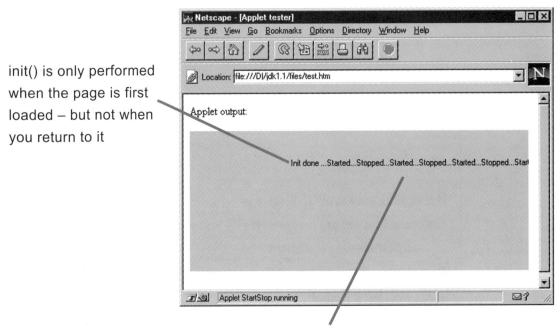.

3 Check the message. You should find that the applet has performed **stop()** and **start()** again.

4 Use the Forward and Back buttons to flip between the pages. The stop…start… message should keep on growing.

5 Reload the test page by giving the Open – File command again. You should find that it has started from scratch, running **init()** and **start()**.

init() is only performed when the page is first loaded – but not when you return to it

Applets run the **stop()** method when you leave their page, and the **start()** method when you return

Text display

If you want to display text, use **drawString()**. This takes three parameters – the text, and the x,y co-ordinates that fix its position. The x,y co-ordinates are measured in pixels – screen dots. They start at the top left of the window, and refer to the *bottom* left of the text. Accurate positioning is a bit tricky as you have to take the size of the font and the length of the text into account. e.g.

```
g.drawString("Hello there", 100, 50);
```

This displays "Hello there", starting 100 pixels from the left and 50 pixels down from the top.

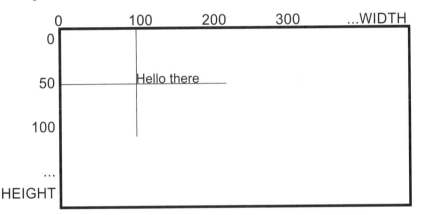

The text can be a literal string (in "quotes"), a **String** variable or any other object or value that can be converted to a String. For example, to display a **StringBuffer** object, you would convert it with the **toString()** method (present in the **StringBuffer** class):

```
g.drawString(sBuffer.toString(), 200, 100);
```

The 'g' is a Graphics object, and is defined in the line:

```
public void paint(Graphics g)
```

Even **paint()** line must have this – you don't have to call it 'g', but you must have a **Graphics** object so that you can call up the drawing methods.

The next two programs demonstrate positioning, and different types of strings. The strings are placed at the corners and centre of the applet. In the first, the default font settings are used.

85

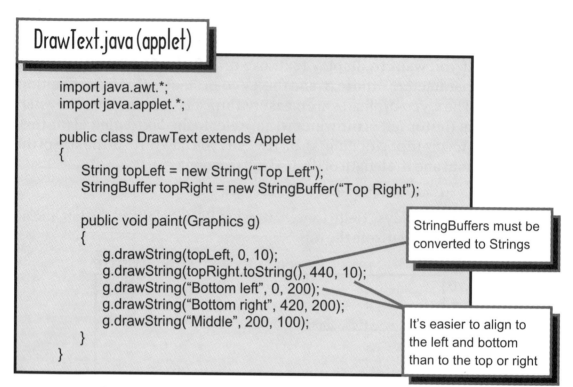

```
DrawText.java (applet)

import java.awt.*;
import java.applet.*;

public class DrawText extends Applet
{
    String topLeft = new String("Top Left");
    StringBuffer topRight = new StringBuffer("Top Right");

    public void paint(Graphics g)
    {
        g.drawString(topLeft, 0, 10);
        g.drawString(topRight.toString(), 440, 10);
        g.drawString("Bottom left", 0, 200);
        g.drawString("Bottom right", 420, 200);
        g.drawString("Middle", 200, 100);
    }
}
```

StringBuffers must be converted to Strings

It's easier to align to the left and bottom than to the top or right

When run through the AppletViewer, the display should be like this:

Applet Viewer: DrawText.class

Applet

Top Left   Top Right

                              Middle

Bottom left   Bottom right

The default font size is 10 point – readable, but not big enough to have much impact

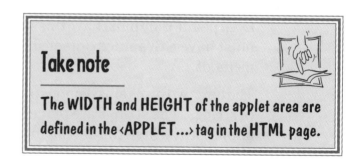

Take note

The WIDTH and HEIGHT of the applet area are defined in the ‹APPLET...› tag in the HTML page.

86

In the second version, the font is increased to 24-point – roughly twice the size – and the x,y co-ordinates have to be adjusted to keep the strings within the applet's area. (For the moment, just accept the Font lines and focus on the fact that if you change the font or size, you may need to adjust the co-ordinates. We will look further into fonts on pages 88 and 158.)

DrawText.java (applet)

```java
import java.awt.*;
import java.applet.*;

public class DrawText1 extends Applet
{
    String topLeft = new String("Top Left");
    StringBuffer topRight = new StringBuffer("Top Right");
    Font header = new Font("SanSerif",Font.BOLD,24);

    public void paint(Graphics g)
    {
        g.setFont(header);
        g.drawString(topLeft, 0, 20);
        g.drawString(topRight.toString(), 375, 20);
        g.drawString("Bottom left", 0, 190);
        g.drawString("Bottom right", 350, 190);
        g.drawString("Middle", 200, 100);
    }
}
```

Define the font...

... and apply it

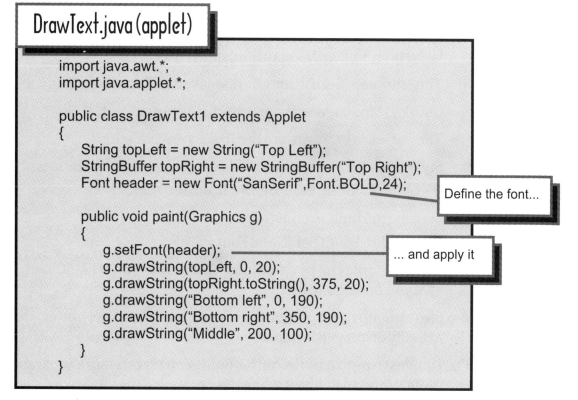

The Font is still the same (SanSerif), but has been increased to 24 point and bold has been turned on

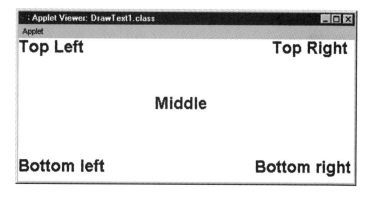

Fonts

Java gives its programmers a remarkable degree of control over the appearance of text – though we only have room to cover the basics in this book.

The **Font** class has three properties:

- **Name** – Java has a small set of standard font names, which are translated into the equivalent fonts on the host machine when a program is executed. The key ones are:

  Helvetica (SanSerif) – may be displayed as Arial

  TimesRoman (Serif) – may be displayed as Times New Roman

  Courier (Monospaced) – may be displayed as Courier New

  The names in brackets are the JDK 1.1 equivalents.

- **Style** – bold, italic or plain. This can be set by the numbers:
  0 = plain, 1 = **bold**, 2 = *italic*, 3 = *bold and italic*

  or using the built-in constants:
  Font.BOLD, Font.ITALIC and Font.PLAIN.

  The constants can be combined 'Font.Bold + Font.ITALIC' will give you *bold, italic* text.

- **Size** – nominally in points, the typesetters' measure, but actually displayed in pixels.

The simplest way to handle fonts is hold each text style in a separate Font object, and to define it when it is created; e.g.

```
Font mainhead  = new Font("TimesRoman",Font.BOLD,36);
```

When you want to set this style, use the **setFont()** method.

```
g.setFont(mainhead);
```

The new font will remain active until you set a new one.

The next program is a simple demonstration of Fonts. Get this running, then play with it – try some different style and size settings.

Fonts.java (applet)

```
import java.awt.*;
import java.applet.*;

public class Fonts extends Applet
{
    Font header  = new Font("TimesRoman",3,24);
    Font subhead  = new Font("Helvetica",Font.BOLD,18);
    Font body  = new Font("Courier",0,14);

    public void paint(Graphics g)
    {
        g.setFont(header);
        g.drawString("Times Roman, a serif font, Bold & Italic, 24 point", 0, 30);
        g.setFont(subhead);
        g.drawString(" Helvetica, a san serif font, Bold, 18 point", 0, 60);
        g.setFont(body);
        g.drawString("Courier, a monospaced font, 14 point",0, 90);
    }
}
```

> Declare and define the Font objects

> Set the Font

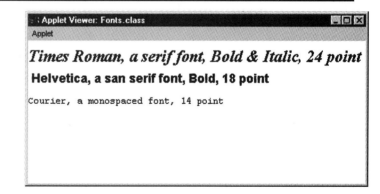

Applet Viewer: Fonts.class

Applet

Times Roman, a serif font, Bold & Italic, 24 point

Helvetica, a san serif font, Bold, 18 point

`Courier, a monospaced font, 14 point`

Take note

There's more about fonts, text size and position on page 158.

Colours

In a computer system colours are made up of red, green and blue light.

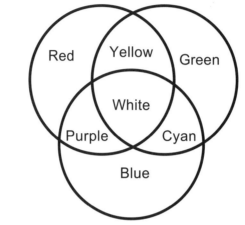

This simple pattern applies where the lights are fully on or off. In practice, each colour can be present at a range of intensities, so that instead of, say, red and green making yellow, they will produce anything from a dark brown through to a pale primrose.

Java offers several ways to handle colour-setting. The simplest defines the intensity of each colour, in the order Red–Green–Blue, on a scale of 0 (off) to 255 (brightest); e.g. 80,64,0 gives a reddy-brown.

In theory, this can give a range of 24 million colours, though how many are actually displayed depends upon the graphics system – you may well find that your screen resolves the colours to a far smaller set.

Color objects and setColor()

Colours are defined through the Color class, e.g.

```
Color   red = new Color(255,0,0);
```

This creates the Color object 'red' and defines it as having red fully on, and green and blue off.

Text and drawn objects (see Chapter 6) are drawn in the current colour, so you must first set the colour before drawing. To do this, use the **setColor()** method, passing to it a Color object:

```
g.setColor(red);
```

This simple demonstration of colour, defines the three primary colours, and mixes a new one – try some combinations of your own.

Colours1.java (applet)

```
import java.awt.*;
import java.applet.*;

public class Colours1 extends Applet
{
    Color   red = new Color(255,0,0);
    Color   green = new Color(0,255,0);
    Color   blue = new Color(0,0,255);
    Color brown = new Color(80,64,0);
    Font sansbold = new Font("Helvetica",Font.BOLD,24);

    public void paint(Graphics g)
    {
        g.setFont(sansbold);
        g.setColor(red);
        g.drawString("Red, RED, R*E*D!", 0, 30);
        g.setColor(green);
        g.drawString("Green, GREEN G_R_E_E_N", 0, 60);
        g.setColor(blue);
        g.drawString("Blue, BLUE, B-L-U-E", 0, 90);
        g.setColor(brown);
        g.drawString("Darkish reddy-brown", 0, 120);
    }
}
```

Give values in the order Red, Green, Blue

A large, bold font shows colours better, but is not essential.

Set the colour

Here's the output – shame this isn't in colour!

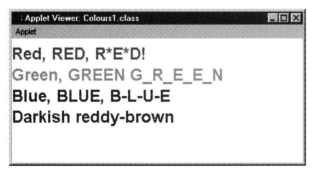

Catching the mouse

If you intend to write any games or interactive graphics programs, you will need to know how to control the mouse. There are several ways to do this, but the simplest use the related methods **mouseDown()**, **mouseUp()** and **mouseDrag()**. These are activated by the appropriate mouse action and pick up the current co-ordinates of the cursor.

```
public boolean mouseDown(Event e, int x, int y)
```

This is executed when the user presses either the left or right button. The *x* and *y* values are the horizontal and vertical positions of the cursor, relative to the top left of the window. If the cursor is in a Canvas, or other component (see the next chapter), then the x,y values are relative to the top left corner of the component. We will ignore the *Event e* parameter here, but this could be examined to find which button was pressed.

The Mouse1 applet responds to a single click by displaying the current co-ordinates, and to a drag action by drawing a line and writing the end co-ordinates at the appropriate places. (For more on line drawing, see Chapter 6.)

Notice the use of the **Boolean** variable *drawing*. The **paint()** method is executed after both a click and a drag action, but you do not want it to attempt to draw a line if the action is only a click.

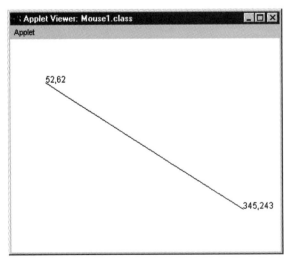

The co-ordinates at the top of the line were written by **mouseDown()**; the line and the lower co-ordinates were added by **mouseDrag()**

Mouse1.java (applet)

```java
import java.awt.*;
import java.applet.Applet;

public class Mouse1 extends Applet
{
    int mx, my;
    int mx1,my1;
    boolean drawing = false;

    public boolean mouseDown(Event e, int x, int y)
    {
        mx = x;
        my = y;
        repaint();
        return(true);
    }

    public boolean mouseDrag(Event e, int x, int y)
    {
        mx1 = x;
        my1 = y;
        drawing = true;
        repaint();
        return(true);
    }

    public void paint(Graphics g)
    {
        g.drawString(mx + "," + my,mx, my);
        if (drawing == true)
        {
            g.drawLine(mx,my,mx1,my1);
            g.drawString(mx1 + "," + my1,mx1, my1);
        }
        drawing = false;
    }
}
```

drawing initially set to *false*

x,y values copied to **mx** and **my** so that they are available in **paint()**

mx1 and **my1** are the new cursor position

drawing set to *true*

only if **drawing** is *true*

The line runs from the position at mouseDown to the current position

drawing turned off again

93

New methods

If you are just writing small applets, the code may well fit neatly into the existing **init()**, **start()**, **paint()** methods. But here, as with applications, large blocks of code are better split into separate methods, called from **start()**, **paint()** or another method, as needed.

Here's a trivial example. The following program writes x,y co-ordinates on the screen. All the code is written within the **paint()** method.

Method1.java (applet)

```java
import java.awt.*;
import java.applet.*;

public class Method1 extends Applet
{
    public void paint(Graphics g)
    {
        int x,y;
        for (y = 25; y < 200 ; y = y+25)
            g.drawString("Y = " + y, 0, y);
        for (x = 50; x < 450 ; x = x+50)
            g.drawString("X = " + x, x, 10);
    }
}
```

Here's the output when run within the 500 x 200 frame of the TEST.HTM page

```
Applet Viewer: Method1.class                                    _ □ ×
Applet
        X= 50   X= 100  X= 150  X= 200  X= 250  X= 300  X= 350  X= 400
Y = 25
Y = 50
Y = 75
Y = 100
Y = 125
Y = 150
Y = 175
```

Here's the same program, with the code rewritten into two methods. Though this version is longer, the individual methods are shorter and more readable.

```java
import java.awt.*;
import java.applet.*;

public class Method1a extends Applet
{
    public void paint(Graphics g)
    {
        vertical(g);
        horizontal(g);
    }
    public void vertical(Graphics g)
    {
        int y;
        for (y = 25; y < 200 ; y = y+25)
            g.drawString("Y = " + y, 0, y);
    }
    public void horizontal(Graphics g)
    {
        int x;
        for (x = 50; x < 450 ; x = x+50)
            g.drawString("X = " + x, x, 10);
    }
}
```

Notice that the new methods take the same **Graphics** parameter as **paint()**.

```java
public void vertical(Graphics g1)
```

This allows them to use the **drawString()** method, and provides a route for passing graphics information between the new methods and **paint()**. When the program reaches this line in **paint()**:

```java
leftright(g);
```

it passes the Graphics object, **g**, to **vertical()**, where the "Y = ..." items are drawn on it.

Applet parameters

You can pass values from the HTML page to your applet. The great thing about this is that it allows you to get different effects from the same applet – without having to rewrite and recompile it. In the simple example given here, the applet slides a message across the window, with both the message and the slide rate controlled by values set in the HTML page.

Values are passed through *parameters*. These are written into the HTML page using <PARAM...> tags, and read into the applet with the **getParameter()** method.

Planning

As both the HTML page and the Java program must be complete and correct before the applet can be tested, it doesn't make any difference which one you do first. Before you start to write either, you should decide which values will be passed, and what names you will give them. In fact, with any program – not just those that use parameters – you should really start by planning it on paper. Any time that you spend on working out the screen layout and thinking through the sequence of events, is time well spent. When you sit down to the keyboard to type in the code, you should have a written outline of the program's structure and a list of the main variables and parameters that it will use.

Here's the plan for this applet, where the aim is to move a message across the screen, starting in the centre and ending on the left edge.

1. Get the text (name = *message*) and the delay limit (name = *limit*, will need *temp* String variable) from the HTML code;
2. Write the message
3. Loop from 200 down to 0 (loop variable = x)
   3.1 delay by running an empty loop – size set by delay limit
   3.2 draw a filled rectangle to wipe out the message
   3.3 rewrite the message

Note: the text written at 2 is erased almost immediately. Could miss out this line.

<PARAM...>

The tags are written within the <APPLET...> block, and take this form:

<PARAM NAME = param_name VALUE = param_value>

- The *param_name* identifies it – you can have any number of parameters in your applet.

- The *param_value* can be text or a number. If the text has more than one word it must be enclosed in "quotes". Miss them out and only the first word will be picked up by the browser, while the AppletViewer won't run at all!

This HTML code defines two parameters – **message** and **limit**.

```
<HTML>
<HEAD>
  <TITLE> Applet tester </TITLE>
</HEAD>
<BODY>
<P>Applet output:</P>
    <P><APPLET CODE="MoveText.class" WIDTH=500 HEIGHT=200>
       <PARAM NAME = message VALUE = "Anyone for Java coffee?">
       <PARAM NAME = limit VALUE = 20000>
    </APPLET></P>
</BODY>
</HTML>
```

getParameter()

This collects the values from the HTML code, and is used like this:

text = getParameter("message");

Two important points to note about **getParameter()**:

- The name of the parameter must be given in "quotes" – though this is not necessary in the HTML code.

- The method always returns a String value. If it is a *number*, it must be converted from a String within the applet. We'll look at this in more detail on page 116, for now, accept that these lines read in the value as a **String** and convert it to an **int**.

```
temp = getParameter("limit");
delayLimit = Integer.parseInt(temp);
```

MoveText.java (applet)

```java
import java.awt.*;
import java.applet.*;

public class MoveText extends Applet
{
    Font header  = new Font("SanSerif",Font.BOLD,24);
    String text;
    String temp;
    int delayLimit;

    public void init()
    {
        text = getParameter("message");
        if (text == null)
            text = "nothing to say";
        temp = getParameter("limit");
        if (temp == null)
            delayLimit = 10000;
        else
            delayLimit = Integer.parseInt(temp);
    }

    public void paint(Graphics g)
    {
        g.setFont(header);
        for (int x = 200; x > 0; x--)
        {
            for (int delay = 0; delay < delayLimit; delay++)
                ;
            g.setColor(new Color(255,255,255));
            g.fillRect(x,80,300,30);
            g.setColor(new Color(0,0,0));
            g.drawString(text, x, 100);
        }
    }
}
```

Defines a big, bold font

Quotes around the PARAM name

Reads the parameter into temp

Converts the **String** into an **int** value

Blank loop to create a delay – even a short one takes many repetitions

Draws a solid rectangle – see Chapter 6 for more on drawn graphics

Creates a temporary Color object to set the colour – use this approach for one-off colour changes, rather than defining a **Color** variable

Here's the (finished) output with the test values. I deliberately used a dark grey rectangle to erase the text, so that its effect would be visible in this demo. In practice, you would want to use the same colour as the applet background. Remember this would be pale grey in a browser, though white in the AppletViewer.

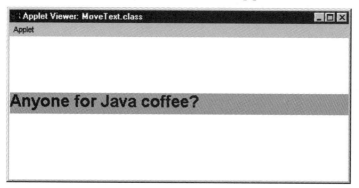

Notice the lines that check for missing or incorrect PARAMs:

```
if (text == null)
    text = "nothing to say";
```

null means that the variable has not been assigned a value. If the PARAM is missing, then "*nothing to say*" is set as a default.

Setting checks and defaults is generally a good idea. It doesn't just guard against error, it also adds to the applet's flexibility – knowing that sensible defaults are available, you only have to write in those PARAMs for which you want to set new values.

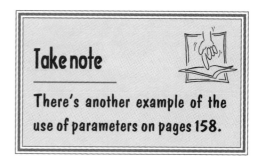

Take note

There's another example of the use of parameters on pages 158.

Exercises

1   Create an applet that will display a message in a large font and a strong colour, then slowly fade the colour away. The program will need a delay loop to slow down the action.

2   Explore font sizes. Write an applet in which the size is held in a variable, which can be controlled by clicking the mouse. Clicks in the upper half of the window should increase the size, and clicks in the lower half reduce it. A message in the centre of the window should display the size value, in text set to that size.

3   Display your name in lights. Draw a few hundred asterisks, or other character, on the window, at random places and in random colours, then write your name over the top. The name should be passed to the applet as a PARAM from the HTML page.

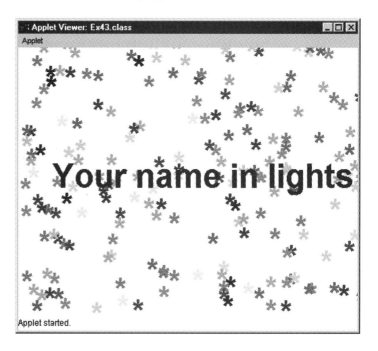

100

5 The user interface

The GUI and its components

The Java AWT gives you all the tools you need for building a standard Windows GUI – sorry, jargon attack, I'll try again in English. The Windows screen, with its buttons, scroll bars, dialog boxes and other display and interactive elements, is referred to as a Graphical User Interface, or GUI (pronounced 'gooey' – and as Java is Object Oriented, it is an OO-GUI or 'ooey-gooey'!) All of the standard components are available within Java.

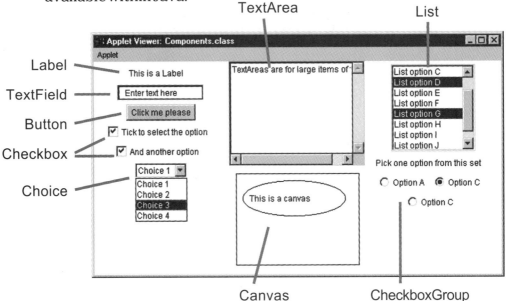

Button

Buttons are for clicking. You can specify their labels, and control what happens when they are clicked.

Canvas

This is an area in which you can draw graphics or text – just as you can in the main window, but a defined space is sometimes more convenient.

Checkbox and CheckbocGroup

These are set up in similar ways, but used differently. With the Checkbox, any number can be selected at the same time. With the related **CheckboxGroup**, only one of each set can be selected.

Choice

These are drop-down lists, from which the user can select one option.

Label

Labels are purely for display. You need them because there is no reliable way to integrate **drawString** items with GUI components. **drawString** items have their positions set by co-ordinates, while GUI components are placed wherever they will fit – with Layouts (page 122) giving you some control.

List

These differ from Choice lists in two respects: several or all of the list items are displayed – with a scrollbar appearing if needed – and more than one item at a time can be selected.

TextField

Use these when you want your user to enter or edit a (short), single line of text. If a user enters more text than the field is designed for, characters are scrolled off the side and cannot easily be accessed again for editing.

TextArea

These are far more flexible that TextFields, with room for an (almost) infinite amount of text and scroll bars for easy reading and editing.

Layouts and Panels

These invisible components give you control over the positioning of elements. In the sample screenshot, three Panels are used to divide the area vertically, and the middle panel uses a Layout to give equal area to the TextArea and Canvas.

Buttons and events

Buttons are probably the easiest – and most useful – GUI components to add to your applets. Here's the code that sets up a button. The same pattern – with variations – is used for all components.

```
Button btnClick = new Button("Click Me");
add(btnClick);
```

The first line creates the button and sets its label text. The **add()** line places the button in the applet window. The code should be written into the **init()** or **start()** method.

Events

In the days before Windows (and other GUIs), event-handling in real time – picking up a user's actions as they happened – was really hard work. Now it is far simpler.

When you move or click the mouse, press a key or interact with an applet in any way, you generate an *event*. Java, through the Windows system, is constantly monitoring the hardware. When it receives an incoming signal, such as a mouse click, it relates this to the current cursor position and screen components, then records the information about what you did and what you did it to, in an event.

There are several methods which handle events. If you write one of these into your program, the method will be executed when an event occurs. With this foundation present, all you have to do is decide what should happen in response to the event – and write the code for it.

To pick up the button's click, you use the action() method, like this:

```
public boolean action(Event evt, Object arg)
{
    ... whatever the button does
    return (true);
}
```

action() has two parameters, both of which can be ignored if you only have one button, and nothing else for the user to play with! What you cannot ignore is the return value. **action()** is a Boolean method. It must end by returning a *true* or *false* value. You don't have to do anything with the value, but it must be returned!

In this first Button example, clicking the button produces a message on screen. Notice the **repaint()** line. This forces execution of the **paint()** method, which would otherwise not happen unless you stopped and started the applet again – i.e. by moving off its page.

But1.java (Applet)

```java
import java.awt.*;
import java.applet.*;

public class But1 extends Applet
{
    Button btnClick;
    String message = "";

    public void init()
    {
        Button btnClick = new Button("Click Me");
        add(btnClick);
    }

    public boolean action(Event evt, Object arg)
    {
        message = "Ouch that really hurt";
        repaint();
        return (true);
    }

    public void paint(Graphics g)
    {
        g.setFont(new Font("SanSerif",Font.ITALIC,30));
        g.setColor(new Color(160,0,0));
        g.drawString(message, 10, 70);

    }
}
```

Java adds the button at the top of the window – you cannot change this

This responds to any event – but a button click is the only possible one in this applet

repaint() cause paint() to run

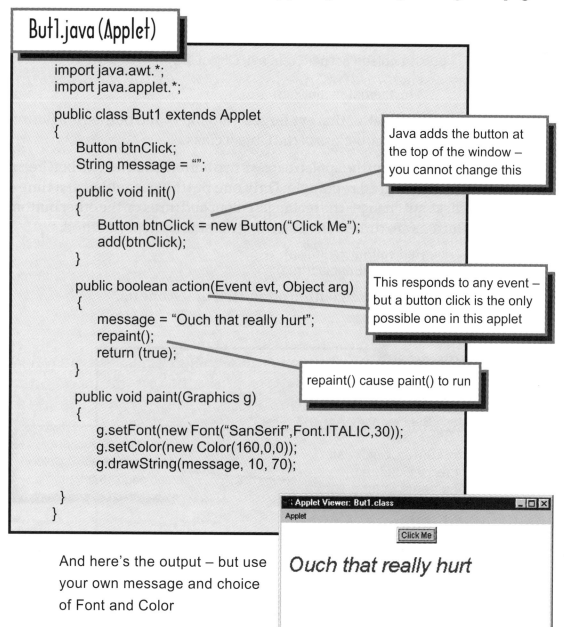

And here's the output – but use your own message and choice of Font and Color

Applet Viewer: But1.class

Applet

Click Me

Ouch that really hurt

Event targets

If you have more that one button, or other component, you have to test the event to see what is happening. This can be handle through the Event parameter of the **action()** method. **Event** contains **target**, an object of the **Object** class which holds the name of the component that was clicked or otherwise affected by the user. All we need to do is compare this with the name of the button, or other component.

```
public boolean action(Event evt, Object arg)
{
    if (evt.target == butRed)
```

It does not matter that **evt.target** is an Object and **butRed** is a Button – Button is a sub-class of the Object class.

In this program the applet displays two buttons, **butRed** and **butGreen**, and a coloured rectangle. Only one button is enabled at a time – clicking it changes the rectangle colour and turns on the other button. Buttons are turned on or off using the setEnabled() method:

```
butRed.setEnabled(false);
butGreen.setEnabled(true);
```

This turns the Red button off and the Green one on.

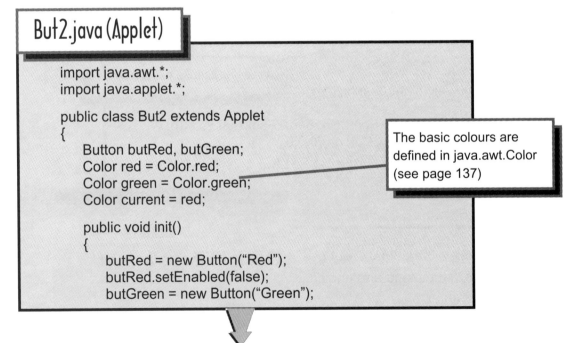

But2.java (Applet)

```
import java.awt.*;
import java.applet.*;

public class But2 extends Applet
{
    Button butRed, butGreen;
    Color red = Color.red;
    Color green = Color.green;
    Color current = red;

    public void init()
    {
        butRed = new Button("Red");
        butRed.setEnabled(false);
        butGreen = new Button("Green");
```

The basic colours are defined in java.awt.Color (see page 137)

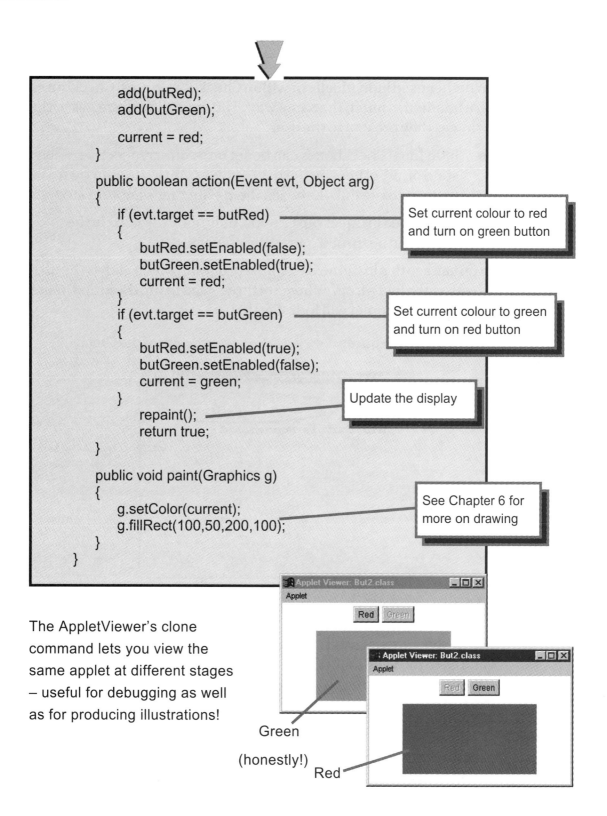

```java
        add(butRed);
        add(butGreen);

        current = red;
    }
    public boolean action(Event evt, Object arg)
    {
        if (evt.target == butRed)
        {
            butRed.setEnabled(false);
            butGreen.setEnabled(true);
            current = red;
        }
        if (evt.target == butGreen)
        {
            butRed.setEnabled(true);
            butGreen.setEnabled(false);
            current = green;
        }
        repaint();
        return true;
    }
    public void paint(Graphics g)
    {
        g.setColor(current);
        g.fillRect(100,50,200,100);
    }
}
```

Set current colour to red and turn on green button

Set current colour to green and turn on red button

Update the display

See Chapter 6 for more on drawing

The AppletViewer's clone command lets you view the same applet at different stages – useful for debugging as well as for producing illustrations!

Applet Viewer: But2.class

Applet

Red   Green

Applet Viewer: But2.class

Applet

Red   Green

Green

(honestly!)   Red

107

Checkboxes and CheckboxGroups

Whether used individually or within CheckboxGroups, Checkboxes are handled in much the same way. The main difference lies in the choices they present to the user.

● Individual Checkboxes can be set on or off, irrespective of the state of any others on the page (unless you write your own code to create links between them – but that's another story).

● When used in CheckboxGroups, only one Checkbox in the group can be turned one at any one time.

You can see this in the next example program, which allows the user to select the font – from a choice of three – and to turn Bold and Italics on or off. The applet will look like this.

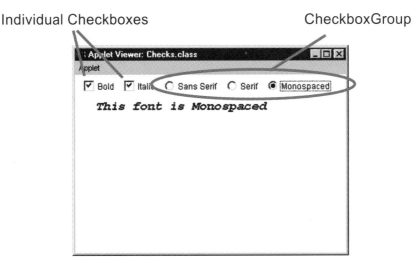

Creating Checkboxes

Checkboxes must exist as objects at program level, as they will be added to the window in the **init()** or **start()** method, and their state checked elsewhere. It is simplest to declare and define them at the same time; for example, this creates the Bold Checkbox:

```
Checkbox fontBold = new Checkbox("Bold",false);
```

Notice that we are using two parameters here. The first sets the label, and the second sets the initial state – *true* for checked (on) or *false* for unchecked. You can omit the state parameter. If you do, the Checkbox is initially off. It can therefore be omitted in this case.

The Checkbox can be added to the window in the **init()** method:

```
add(fontBold);
```

When the Checkbox is part of a group, the CheckboxGroup must be created first.

```
CheckboxGroup fontName= new CheckboxGroup();
Checkbox sans = new Checkbox("Sans Serif", fontName, true);
```

And now you see why – the CheckboxGroup's name is the second parameter used in setting up the Checkbox. The true/false state is now the third parameter, and – of course – only one of the group can be set to *true*.

Checking Checkboxes

When the user clicks on a Checkbox, this can be picked up by the general purpose **action()** method. You could check the Event target object, to see which box had been clicked, but it is probably simpler to do a quick check on the state of all boxes.

Different styles of test are needed for individual Checkboxes and for those in CheckboxGroups.

Each individual Checkbox should be tested to see if it is true or false – the getState() method will tell us this:

```
if(fontBold.getState()== true)
```

You would normally want to set a variable to carry the result to another part of the program. This variable could be a Boolean, in which case you could use lines of the type:

```
boldOn = fontBold.getState();
```

This simply copies the state to the variable, which is then tested elsewhere in the program. In the example, **int** variables are used. *bold* is set to 1 if the Bold Checkbox is on, and *italic* is set to 2 if its Checkbox is on. These are, of course, the values needed to set the font style to bold and italic.

With the CheckboxGroup, the question is which Checkbox is selected. We could test the state of each, like this:

```
if (sans.getState() == true)
    fName = "Sans Serif";
else if (serif.getState() == true)
    fName = "Serif";
else
    fName = "Monospaced";
```

After working through this set, the String *fName* has the name of the font, ready for use in the **setFont()** line in paint().

Alternatively, we can use the method **getSelected Checkbox()**, comparing it with the names of the Checkboxes in the set:

```
if (fontName.getSelectedCheckbox() == sans)
    fName = "Sans Serif";
else if (fontName.getSelectedCheckbox() == serif)
    fName = "Serif";
else
    fName = "Monospaced";
```

Here's the full program.

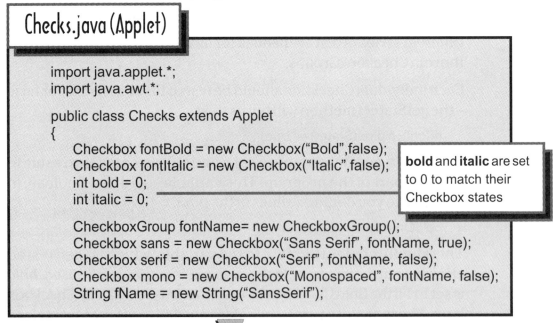

Checks.java (Applet)

```
import java.applet.*;
import java.awt.*;

public class Checks extends Applet
{
    Checkbox fontBold = new Checkbox("Bold",false);
    Checkbox fontItalic = new Checkbox("Italic",false);
    int bold = 0;
    int italic = 0;

    CheckboxGroup fontName= new CheckboxGroup();
    Checkbox sans = new Checkbox("Sans Serif", fontName, true);
    Checkbox serif = new Checkbox("Serif", fontName, false);
    Checkbox mono = new Checkbox("Monospaced", fontName, false);
    String fName = new String("SansSerif");
```

bold and **italic** are set to 0 to match their Checkbox states

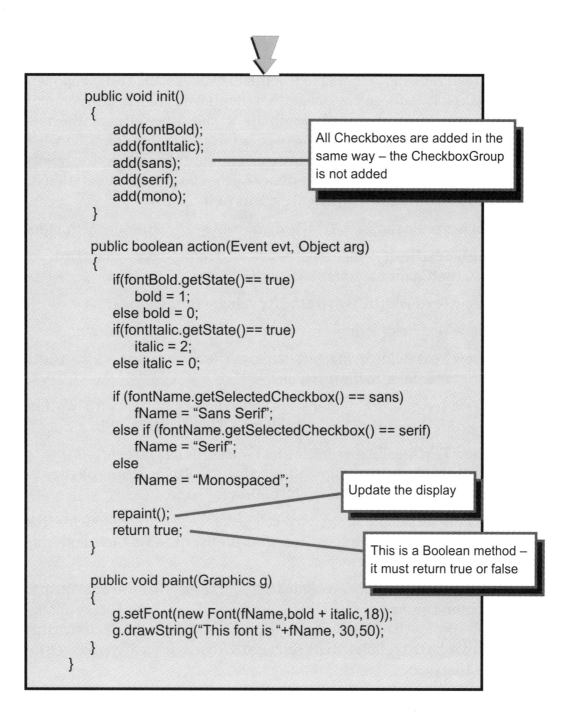

```
public void init()
{
    add(fontBold);
    add(fontItalic);
    add(sans);
    add(serif);
    add(mono);
}

public boolean action(Event evt, Object arg)
{
    if(fontBold.getState()== true)
        bold = 1;
    else bold = 0;
    if(fontItalic.getState()== true)
        italic = 2;
    else italic = 0;

    if (fontName.getSelectedCheckbox() == sans)
        fName = "Sans Serif";
    else if (fontName.getSelectedCheckbox() == serif)
        fName = "Serif";
    else
        fName = "Monospaced";

    repaint();
    return true;
}

public void paint(Graphics g)
{
    g.setFont(new Font(fName,bold + italic,18));
    g.drawString("This font is "+fName, 30,50);
}
}
```

All Checkboxes are added in the same way – the CheckboxGroup is not added

Update the display

This is a Boolean method – it must return true or false

Text Components

TextFields and TextAreas are both sub-classes of the Text Component class. This doesn't just mean that they have a great deal in common – sub-classes contain the methods of their super-classes (the ones that they are derived from) as well as their own special ones. So, when you are looking through the documentation for methods to use with a TextField or TextArea, step back up the class hierarchy, and have a look at the Text Component class as well.

When setting up a new TextField, you can use any of these constructors:

new TextField() which must be followed somewhere by a **setText()** or **setColumns()** method to fix its size;

new TextField(*int*) where the *int* value sets its width;

new TextField(*String*) creates a field displaying the *String;*

new TextField(*String*, *int*) displays the *String*, but sets the width according to the *int* value.

TextAreas have a similar set of constructors, though with two ints, setting the size in rows and columns. There is also a fifth:

new TextArea(String, int, int, int) where the last *int* controls the scrollbars: 1 turns off the vertical scroll bar; 2 turns off the horizontal and 3 turns off both scrollbars.

The first example shows a typical use for these two components. The TextField collects a short item from the user; the TextArea collects a longer, multi-line entry.

Notice the prompts – you must tell your users what you want them to enter. The *email* TextField is accompanied by a Label. For the *details*, the prompt has been written into the TextArea, then selected so that it can be easily deleted and replaced. Either approach can be used for either type.

Texts1.java (Applet)

```java
import java.applet.*;
import java.awt.*;

public class Texts1 extends Applet
{
    TextField email;
    TextArea details;

    public void init()
    {
        add(new Label("Your e-mail address"));
        email = new TextField(40);
        add(email);
        details = new TextArea("Enter your name and address here",6,40);
        add(details);
        details.selectAll();
        validate();
    }
}
```

> In the completed applet, these values would be picked up and used elsewhere

> Label to prompt the user

> The initial text could be a default value or a prompt

> **selectAll()** is a Text Component method – you must **add()** the component before you select its text.

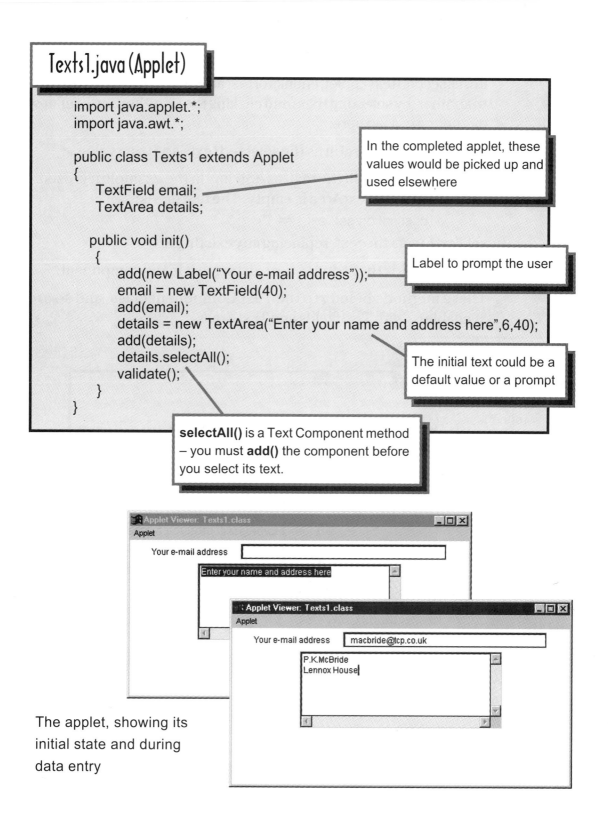

The applet, showing its initial state and during data entry

Working with text

In this second text applet, chunks of text are copied from one TextArea to another, by selecting them and clicking the Copy button. Four new methods are used here:

getSelectedText() returns the selected text as a String value

getText() returns all the text, as a String. In the example it is used to check if a TextArea is empty. The test line is:

```
if (destination.getText() == "")
```

setText() sets the text, replacing any existing text

append() adds the String to the existing text in the component.

These methods belong to the **Text Component** class, and so are available to both TextFields and TextAreas.

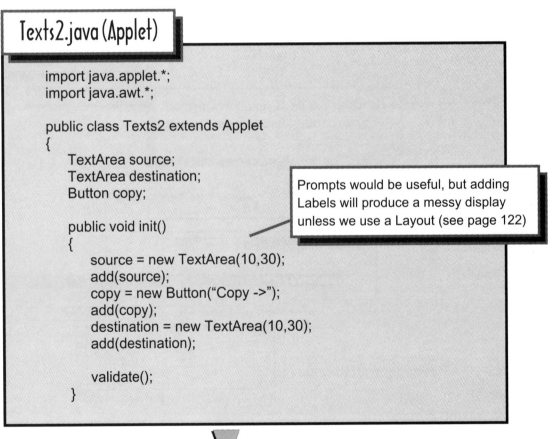

Texts2.java (Applet)

```java
import java.applet.*;
import java.awt.*;

public class Texts2 extends Applet
{
    TextArea source;
    TextArea destination;
    Button copy;

    public void init()
    {
        source = new TextArea(10,30);
        add(source);
        copy = new Button("Copy ->");
        add(copy);
        destination = new TextArea(10,30);
        add(destination);

        validate();
    }
```

> Prompts would be useful, but adding Labels will produce a messy display unless we use a Layout (see page 122)

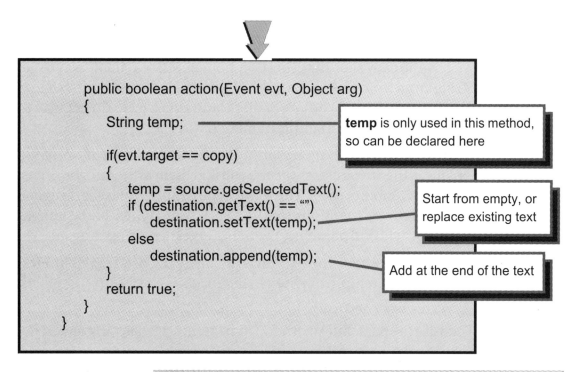

```
public boolean action(Event evt, Object arg)
{
    String temp;

    if(evt.target == copy)
    {
        temp = source.getSelectedText();
        if (destination.getText() == "")
            destination.setText(temp);
        else
            destination.append(temp);
    }
    return true;
}
}
```

temp is only used in this method, so can be declared here

Start from empty, or replace existing text

Add at the end of the text

Text selected on the left, ready for copying across

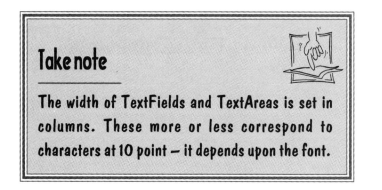

Take note

The width of TextFields and TextAreas is set in columns. These more or less correspond to characters at 10 point — it depends upon the font.

Working with numbers

We have already seen that Text Components offer a simple way to get String input from a user. Getting a number value is not quite so easy. Text Components produce Strings, and there is no direct way to convert a String into a simple number data type.

If you want a method for converting Strings to numbers, it's no good looking in the String class, but you will find them in the Integer, Short, Float and Double classes. These are 'type wrapper' classes designed to provide extra functions for the related data types. In the Integer class, you will find **parseInt()**, which converts a String to an int.

This is what we have to do to get an **int** value out of a **TextField**. First get the String, *temp*, from the TextField, *entry*.

```
temp = entry.getText();
```

Then use the **parseInt()** method, from the **Integer** class, to convert the String to the int, *number*.

```
number = Integer.parseInt(temp);
```

The following program demonstrates getting number values out of a TextField. It invites the user to guess a random number, giving "Too high" and "Too low" messages until it is guessed correctly.

When run through the AppletViewer, the applet should look like this:

Guess.java (applet)

```java
import java.awt.*;
import java.applet.*;

public class Guess extends Applet
{
    Button btnClick;
    TextField entry;
    Label prompt;
    String temp;
    int x = (int)(java.lang.Math.random() * 100);
    int number;

    public void init()
    {
        prompt = new Label("Guess the number");
        add(prompt);
        entry = new TextField(10);
        add(entry);
        btnClick = new Button("Check your guess");
        add(btnClick);
    }

    public boolean action(Event evt, Object arg)
    {
        temp = entry.getText();
        number = Integer.parseInt(temp);
        if (x > number)
            prompt.setText("Too low. Try again");
        else if (x < number)
            prompt.setText("Too high. Try again");
        else
            prompt.setText("Found it!");
        return (true);
    }
}
```

Copy the field's text into **temp**

Convert **temp** to an int value

Choices and Lists

A Choice object is a drop-down list, from which the user can select one item. A List object is displayed in full, or in a scrollable box, and the user can normally select several items at once. So, although the two types of Components are set up with similar routines, a different approach is needed for checking and recording selections.

addItem()

With a CheckboxGroup, each of its Checkboxes is a separate object which must be created and added individually. The opposite applies to Choices and Lists. A Choice (or a List) is a single Component, and its options are an integral part of it. At its simplest, a Choice could be set up like this:

```
Choice c = new Choice();
c.addItem("Option 1");
c.addItem("Option 2");
add(c);
```

A List would be set up in the same way.

The index

Options are displayed on screen, in the order of their addItem() lines. They are also stored within the Choice in that order, and can be identified by their *index* value, starting from 0. You can use the index to set defaults. For example, to set "Option 2" as the initial selection, you would use the **select()** method, like this:

```
c.select(1);
```

After the user has made a choice, you can read the index value to find out what it was:

```
chosen = c.getSelectedIndex();
```

An index is rarely much use in its raw form. You normally would want to use it to select an action or set another variable. This could be done through an **if... else...** block, as we did with the CheckboxGroup in the last program. The index could also be used to drive a **switch** block:

```
switch (c.getSelectedIndex())
{
    case 0 : ...action for 0...; break;
    case 1 : ...action for 1...; break;
    ...
}
```

There's another approach which can prove very convenient. Think for a moment about arrays. An array is a set of elements, each of which can be identified by a subscript – in effect, the same structure as a Choice or List.

The next program allows its users to specify their own PC. It has a Choice, *micro*, which lists processors. In the **action()** method you will find these lines:

```
p = micro.getSelectedIndex();
...
spec.setText("Pentium "+procType[p] + " at £" + procCost[p]+ "\n");
```

The index is assigned to *p*, which is then used to pull corresponding values from the *procType[]* and *procCost[]* arrays – these are set up in **init()** and hold the type number and price of the processors.

getSelectedIndex is of little use with a List, where several items can be selected at once. (Though you can force single item selection with **setMultipleMode(false)** .)

To find out if an item has been selected, use the **isIndexSelected()** method. Give this the index number of the item, and it will return *true* if the item is selected. In the example, this is used to pick values from the *peripheral[]* array. The names of selected peripherals are then added to the *spec* TextArea.

```
for(int loop = 0; loop < 8; loop++)
    if(parts.isIndexSelected(loop) == true)
        spec.append(peripheral[loop] + "\n");
```

Look at the program, and you will see that this selection is only done when the "Done" button is pressed – not when an item is selected. Why is this?

Lists.java (Applet)

```java
import java.applet.*;
import java.awt.*;

public class Lists extends Applet
{
    Choice micro;
    List parts;
    Button done;
    TextArea spec;

    int[] procType = new int[4];
    float[] procCost = new float[4];
    int p = 0;
    String[] peripheral = new String[8];

    public void init()
    {
        micro = new Choice();
        micro.addItem("P133");
        micro.addItem("P150");
        micro.addItem("P166");
        micro.addItem("P200");
        micro.select(0);
        add(micro);

        procType[0] = 133;
        procCost[0] = 85;
        procType[1] = 150;
        procCost[1] = 95;
        procType[2] = 166;
        procCost[2] = 135;
        procType[3] = 200;
        procCost[3] = 165;

        peripheral[0] = "CD-ROM";
        peripheral[1] = "Sound card";
        peripheral[2] = "Speakers";
        peripheral[3] = "Tape Drive";
        peripheral[4] = "Zip Drive";
        peripheral[5] = "Modem";
        peripheral[6] = "Extra 16Mb RAM";
        peripheral[7] = "1.2Gb Hard Drive";
```

The GUI Components

Processor types and prices

To store the **micro** index

Peripherals array

Processor Choice ...

... and the values for the related arrays

Peripheral names – stored here, then...

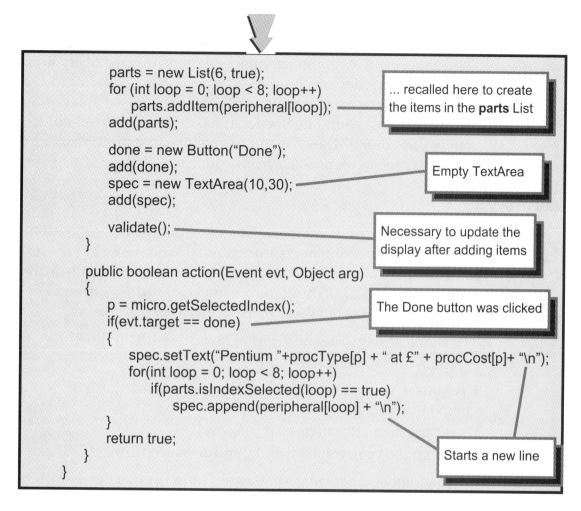

```
            parts = new List(6, true);
            for (int loop = 0; loop < 8; loop++)
                parts.addItem(peripheral[loop]);
            add(parts);

            done = new Button("Done");
            add(done);
            spec = new TextArea(10,30);
            add(spec);

            validate();
        }
    public boolean action(Event evt, Object arg)
    {
        p = micro.getSelectedIndex();
        if(evt.target == done)
        {
            spec.setText("Pentium "+procType[p] + " at £" + procCost[p]+ "\n");
            for(int loop = 0; loop < 8; loop++)
                if(parts.isIndexSelected(loop) == true)
                    spec.append(peripheral[loop] + "\n");
        }
        return true;
    }
}
```

... recalled here to create the items in the **parts** List

Empty TextArea

Necessary to update the display after adding items

The Done button was clicked

Starts a new line

The applet in use. Your display may well look different. Unless you set a layout (see next page) the system uses the Flow Layout, which places components one after the other across the screen, wrapping to a second line if necessary.

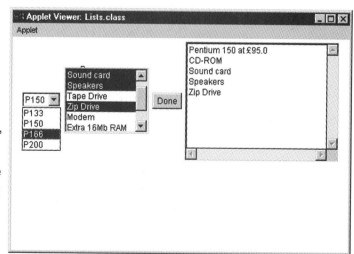

Layouts

The arrangement of components depends upon the Layout. If you do not specify it, the default Flow Layout is used – and this is fine where you have only a few components. With more complex displays, you should set the layout. The Border and Grid layouts are simple to manage, and though they have some significant restrictions, using them with Panels (see page 125) can produce well-balanced displays.

BorderLayout()

This can take up to five components – four around the edges, and one in the centre. The components are expanded (or shrunk) as necessary to fill the space allocated to them, and you cannot control this. In the following example, all the components are buttons, as they show clearly the resizing, but they could be any other GUI objects.

The simplest way to define a Border layout is with this line:

    setLayout(new BorderLayout());

If required, you can set the horizontal and vertical gaps between components using this variation:

    setLayout(new BorderLayout(*hgap*,*vgap*));

The *hgap* and *vgap* values are ints, and measured in pixels.

When adding components to the layout, you must specify where they go, using the keywords "North", "South", "East", "West" and "Center". This places a Button, with the label "North", at the top of the layout:

    add(new Button("NORTH"),"North");

Border layouts can take a maximum of five objects, but do not have to take this many. A layout that just used "North" and "Center" would give you one large main area and a thin component across the top.

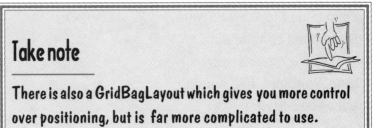

Take note

There is also a GridBagLayout which gives you more control over positioning, but is far more complicated to use.

122

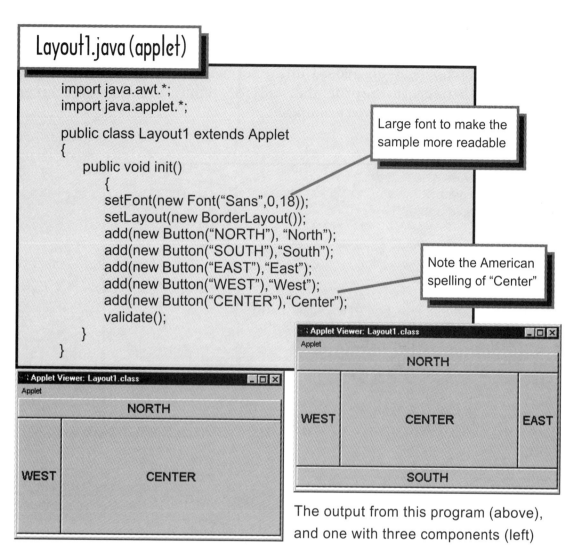

Layout1.java (applet)

```java
import java.awt.*;
import java.applet.*;

public class Layout1 extends Applet
{
    public void init()
        {
        setFont(new Font("Sans",0,18));
        setLayout(new BorderLayout());
        add(new Button("NORTH"), "North");
        add(new Button("SOUTH"),"South");
        add(new Button("EAST"),"East");
        add(new Button("WEST"),"West");
        add(new Button("CENTER"),"Center");
        validate();
        }
}
```

Large font to make the sample more readable

Note the American spelling of "Center"

The output from this program (above), and one with three components (left)

GridLayout()

The Grid layout makes all components the same size and arranges them in rows and columns – and if one row has fewer components than the rest, it will have blanks at the end. You specify the number of rows and columns, and the gaps between them. e.g.

    setLayout(new GridLayout(2,3));

Creates a grid of 2 rows and 3 columns.

    setLayout(new GridLayout(4,2,10,5));

Creates a grid or 4 rows and 2 columns, with a horizontal gap of 10 pixels and a vertical gap of 5 pixels between components.

Components are added with the normal add() method, and are added to the grid in the order that you write them into your code. You can see that in the next example.

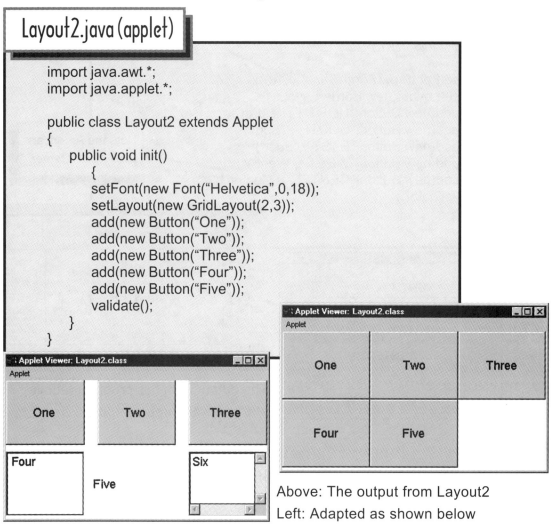

Layout2.java (applet)

```java
import java.awt.*;
import java.applet.*;

public class Layout2 extends Applet
{
    public void init()
    {
        setFont(new Font("Helvetica",0,18));
        setLayout(new GridLayout(2,3));
        add(new Button("One"));
        add(new Button("Two"));
        add(new Button("Three"));
        add(new Button("Four"));
        add(new Button("Five"));
        validate();
    }
}
```

Above: The output from Layout2
Left: Adapted as shown below

Create some space between the components by setting gap values:

```java
setLayout(new GridLayout(2,3,20,10));
```

Delete the lines that create buttons Four and Five, and insert these:

```java
add(new TextField("Four"));
add(new Label("Five"));
add(new TextArea("Six"));
```

Panels

Panels are invisible and largely inactive, but essential to good screen displays. This is because you can place Panels within layouts, and set layouts within panels. You can also mix panels and other components in a layout – the next program has Panels at the West and South, and a Canvas at the Center. Here's its plan, showing the arrangement of panels and layouts. Compare it with the screen display.

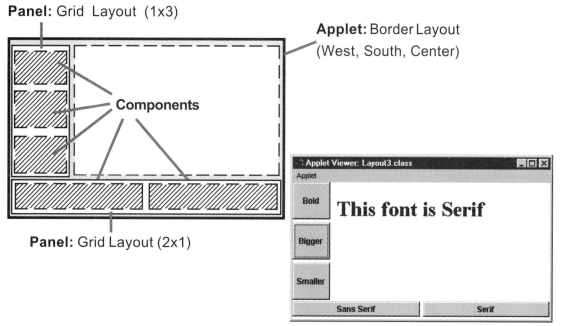

Panel: Grid Layout (1x3)

Applet: Border Layout
(West, South, Center)

Components

Panel: Grid Layout (2x1)

To create a panelled layout, start by setting the layout for the applet:

```
setLayout(new BorderLayout());
```

Then create a panel, and set its layout – and note that you must prefix **setLayout()** with the panel's name.

```
Panel p1 = new Panel();
p1.setLayout(new GridLayout(2,5));
```

Components are created and added to the panel, as to the main applet, except that again you must prefix **add()** with the panel's name.

```
p1.add(new Label("Control Bar"));
```

When the panel is complete, add it to the main layout, just as you would add any other component.

```
add(p1, "South");
```

```
import java.awt.*;
import java.applet.*;

public class Layout3 extends Applet
{
    Panel fnames,styles;
    Button sans,serif;
    Button bold,bigger,smaller;
    SampleCanvas sample;
    String fName = new String("SansSerif");
    int fBold = 0;
    int fSize = 12;

public void init()
{
    setFont(new Font("Sans",Font.BOLD,12));
    setLayout(new BorderLayout());

    fnames = new Panel();
    fnames.setLayout(new GridLayout(1,2,5,10));
    sans = new Button("Sans Serif");
    fnames.add(sans);
    serif = new Button("Serif");
    fnames.add(serif);
    add(fnames, "South");

    styles = new Panel();
    styles.setLayout(new GridLayout(3,1,10,5));
    bold = new Button("Bold");
    styles.add(bold);
    bigger = new Button("Bigger");
    styles.add(bigger);
    smaller = new Button("Smaller");
    styles.add(smaller);
    add(styles, "West");

    sample = new SampleCanvas();
    add(sample,"Center");
    validate();
}
```

SampleCanvas redefines the **Canvas** class so that we can redraw it in our program – a simple **Canvas** would not work

Variables so that we can adjust the Font settings

Set the main layout

Set the panel layout

Add components to the panel

Add the panel to the display

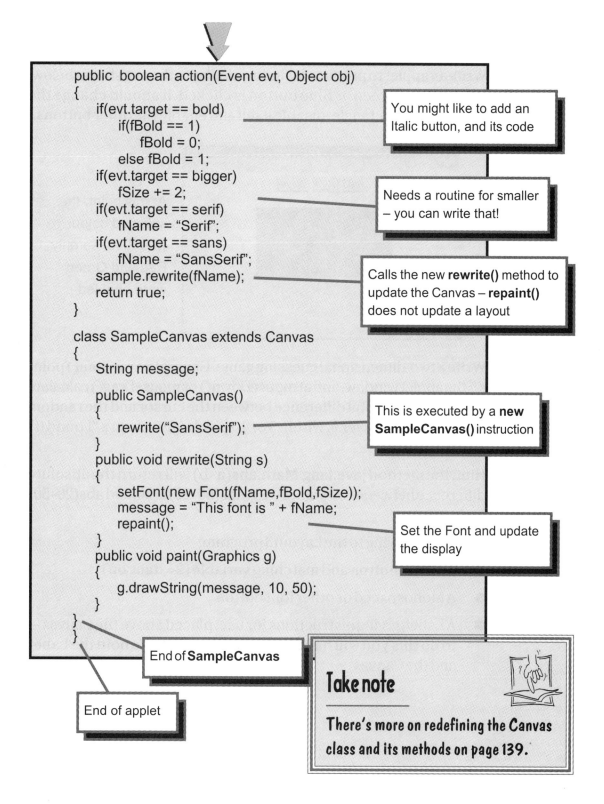

```
public boolean action(Event evt, Object obj)
{
    if(evt.target == bold)
        if(fBold == 1)
            fBold = 0;
        else fBold = 1;
    if(evt.target == bigger)
        fSize += 2;
    if(evt.target == serif)
        fName = "Serif";
    if(evt.target == sans)
        fName = "SansSerif";
    sample.rewrite(fName);
    return true;
}

class SampleCanvas extends Canvas
{
    String message;

    public SampleCanvas()
    {
        rewrite("SansSerif");
    }
    public void rewrite(String s)
    {
        setFont(new Font(fName,fBold,fSize));
        message = "This font is " + fName;
        repaint();
    }
    public void paint(Graphics g)
    {
        g.drawString(message, 10, 50);
    }
}
}
```

You might like to add an Italic button, and its code

Needs a routine for smaller – you can write that!

Calls the new **rewrite()** method to update the Canvas – **repaint()** does not update a layout

This is executed by a **new SampleCanvas()** instruction

Set the Font and update the display

End of **SampleCanvas**

End of applet

Take note

There's more on redefining the Canvas class and its methods on page 139.

127

Exercises

1 Write an applet to produce a window similar to the one shown below. When a Red, Green or Blue button is clicked, it should change the colour of the rectangle, disable itself and enable the other buttons.

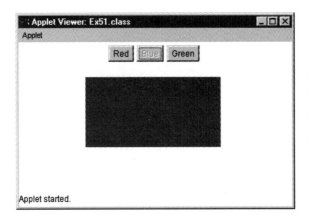

At this point, the selected colour was Blue, so only Red and Green were enabled

2 Write a two-dimensional guessing game. Generate a random() point on the applet window, and at **mouseDown()** or **mouseDrag()** calculate and display the total difference between the cursor and the random point. When the user is within 5 or 10 pixels, give them a "Found it" message.

Hint: the method **java.lang.Math.abs(a-b)** will return the absolute difference between two values – e.g. **abs(50-20)** is 30, and **abs(20-50)** is also 30.

3 Add the following to the Layout3 program:

● An Italic button and matching variable (2 = italic on)

● A Monospaced or other font button

● A Label, giving instructions for use, placed above the Canvas – to do this you will have to create a new Panel to hold the Label and the Canvas.

6 Graphics

Lines

The Graphics class contains several drawing methods. They are fairly limited – lines are one pixel thick, and the object is always drawn in the current colour – but serve well for diagrams and for enhancing text, and can even be used for simple animation.

Drawing is best done within **paint()**. You can draw directly onto the applet, or onto a Canvas. Drawing on Canvases raises problems that we touched on in the last section. It is dealt with on page 139.

drawLine()

This draws a line between two points, with their co-ordinates given in pixels (counting from the top left).

```
g.drawLine(0,0,100,50)
```

This draws a thin line from the top left corner to a point 100 pixels from the left and 50 pixels down. If a thicker line is needed, you can draw more lines alongside. You can see this in the next example.

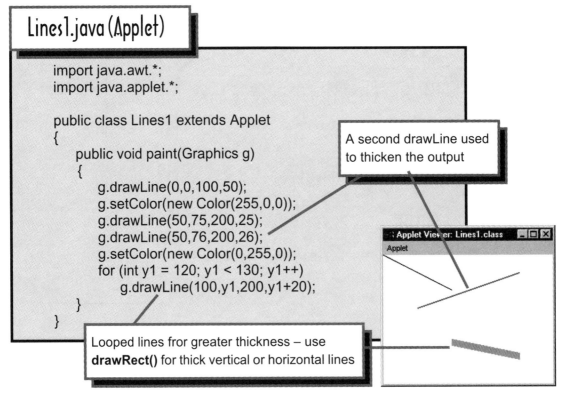

Lines1.java (Applet)

```java
import java.awt.*;
import java.applet.*;

public class Lines1 extends Applet
{
    public void paint(Graphics g)
    {
        g.drawLine(0,0,100,50);
        g.setColor(new Color(255,0,0));
        g.drawLine(50,75,200,25);
        g.drawLine(50,76,200,26);
        g.setColor(new Color(0,255,0));
        for (int y1 = 120; y1 < 130; y1++)
            g.drawLine(100,y1,200,y1+20);
    }
}
```

A second drawLine used to thicken the output

Looped lines fror greater thickness – use **drawRect()** for thick vertical or horizontal lines

Applet Viewer: Lines1.class

Applet

130

The next program creates a simple animated effect – a line sweeping round in a circle. Here's the maths behind the circle routine:

Java measures angles in *Radians*, and 2xPI (6.28) radians equals 360 degrees. At any angle, the radius can be treated as the hypothenuse of a triangle, and the other two sides give the x,y values of a point on the circumference.

x = (int)(java.lang.Math.cos(angle)* 100) + 150;

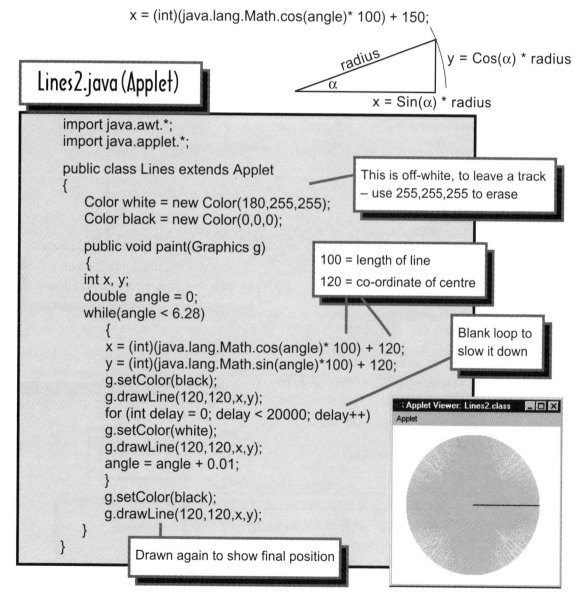

Lines2.java (Applet)

radius

y = Cos(α) * radius

α

x = Sin(α) * radius

```java
import java.awt.*;
import java.applet.*;

public class Lines extends Applet
{
    Color white = new Color(180,255,255);
    Color black = new Color(0,0,0);

    public void paint(Graphics g)
    {
    int x, y;
    double  angle = 0;
    while(angle < 6.28)
        {
        x = (int)(java.lang.Math.cos(angle)* 100) + 120;
        y = (int)(java.lang.Math.sin(angle)*100) + 120;
        g.setColor(black);
        g.drawLine(120,120,x,y);
        for (int delay = 0; delay < 20000; delay++)
        g.setColor(white);
        g.drawLine(120,120,x,y);
        angle = angle + 0.01;
        }
        g.setColor(black);
        g.drawLine(120,120,x,y);
    }
}
```

This is off-white, to leave a track – use 255,255,255 to erase

100 = length of line

120 = co-ordinate of centre

Blank loop to slow it down

Applet Viewer: Lines2.class
Applet

Drawn again to show final position

131

Rectangles

There are two rectangle methods: **drawRect()** draws an outline, and **fillRect()** produces a solid block. Both must be given the co-ordinates of the top left corner and the size of the rectangle:

> g.fillRect(50,150,200,100);

This draws a block, 200 pixels wide and 100 high, starting at 50, 150.

drawRect() lines are thin. If you want a thick frame, use a loop or place one **fillRect()** block within another. These are illustrated below.

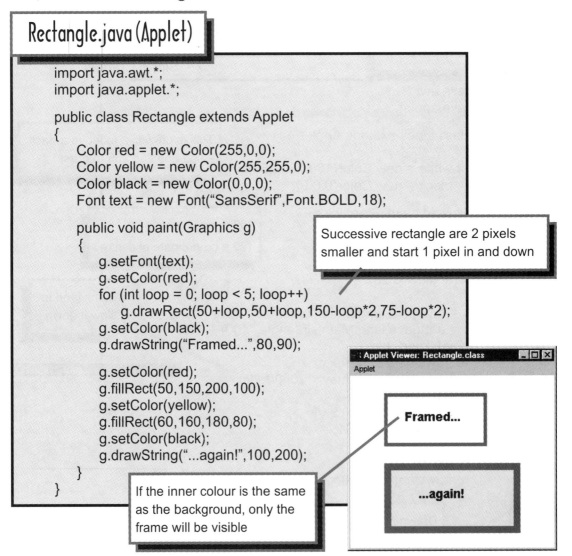

Rectangle.java (Applet)

```java
import java.awt.*;
import java.applet.*;

public class Rectangle extends Applet
{
    Color red = new Color(255,0,0);
    Color yellow = new Color(255,255,0);
    Color black = new Color(0,0,0);
    Font text = new Font("SansSerif",Font.BOLD,18);

    public void paint(Graphics g)
    {
        g.setFont(text);
        g.setColor(red);
        for (int loop = 0; loop < 5; loop++)
            g.drawRect(50+loop,50+loop,150-loop*2,75-loop*2);
        g.setColor(black);
        g.drawString("Framed...",80,90);

        g.setColor(red);
        g.fillRect(50,150,200,100);
        g.setColor(yellow);
        g.fillRect(60,160,180,80);
        g.setColor(black);
        g.drawString("...again!",100,200);
    }
}
```

Successive rectangle are 2 pixels smaller and start 1 pixel in and down

If the inner colour is the same as the background, only the frame will be visible

Applet Viewer: Rectangle.class

Applet

Framed...

...again!

Ovals

If you want ovals (and circles are just regular ovals), use the **drawOval()** or **fillOval()**. These follow the same pattern as those for rectangles. You do *not* define them by their centre and radius, but by the top left corner and size of the rectangle that would just enclose them. You can see this in the demonstration program, where the ovals are drawn with their matching rectangles.

Ovals.java (Applet)

```
import java.awt.*;
import java.applet.*;

public class Ovals extends Applet
{
    Color grey = new Color(160,160,160);
    Color black = new Color(0,0,0);

    public void paint(Graphics g)
    {
        g.drawRect(10,10,150,100);
        g.setColor(grey);
        g.fillOval(10,10,150,100);

        g.fillRect(180,40,100,100);
        g.setColor(black);
        g.fillOval(180,40,100,100);
        g.setColor(grey);
        g.fillOval(200,60,60,60);
    }
}
```

The parameters are given in exactly the same way for ovals and rectangles

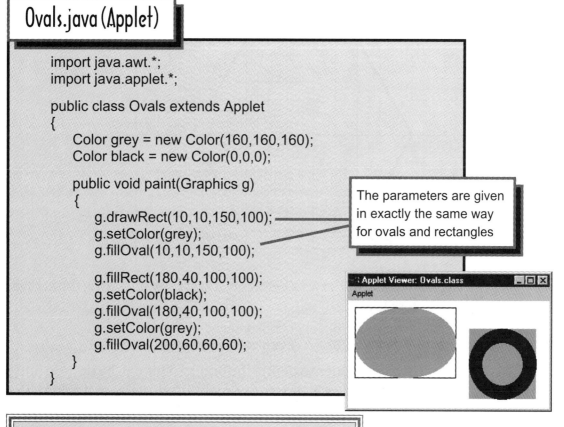

Tip

When designing with ovals, it may be easier to place them accurately if you think in terms of centre and radius, then convert these to the top left and size parameters.

Polygons

You can use **drawPolygon()** and **fillPolygon()** to produce anything from triangles to complex regular and irregular shapes with any number of sides. The shapes are defined by the co-ordinates of their vertices, which are written into a pair of matching **int** arrays.

If you want to get a reasonably accurate image, you will find it useful to draw it on squared paper and read off the co-ordinates.

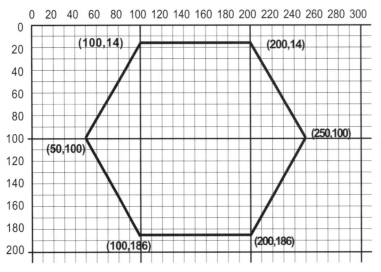

The next example draws a hexagon. It starts by declaring the arrays, at the class level:

```
int[ ] x = new int[6];      // horizontal co-ordinates
int[ ] y = new int[6];      // vertical co-ordinates
```

Next, it assigns values to define the points. This can be done in **init()** or **start()**. The code will be more readable if you write matching pairs of statements on one line – ending each with a semi-colon.

```
x[0] = 100; y[0] = 145;
```

Remember that in a 6-element array, the subscripts run from 0 to 5.

The drawing methods should be called from within **paint()**. They take as parameters the names of the two arrays and the number of points.

```
g.drawPolygon(x,y,6)
```

Note that the arrays are identified simply by their names – the [ ] brackets have no place here!

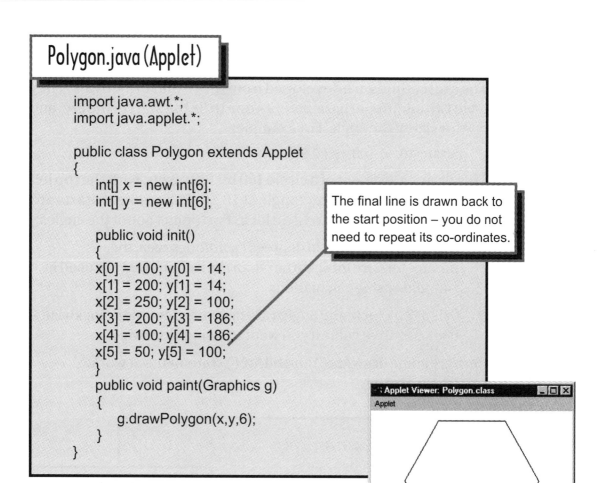

Polygon.java (Applet)

```java
import java.awt.*;
import java.applet.*;

public class Polygon extends Applet
{
    int[] x = new int[6];
    int[] y = new int[6];

    public void init()
    {
    x[0] = 100; y[0] = 14;
    x[1] = 200; y[1] = 14;
    x[2] = 250; y[2] = 100;
    x[3] = 200; y[3] = 186;
    x[4] = 100; y[4] = 186;
    x[5] = 50; y[5] = 100;
    }
    public void paint(Graphics g)
    {
        g.drawPolygon(x,y,6);
    }
}
```

The final line is drawn back to the start position – you do not need to repeat its co-ordinates.

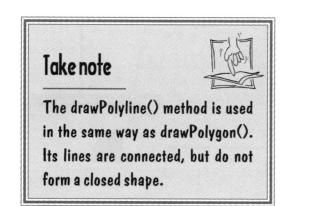

Take note

The drawPolyline() method is used in the same way as drawPolygon(). Its lines are connected, but do not form a closed shape.

Arcs

The arc methods are developed from those that draw ovals. They have two additional parameters – one to fix the start of the arc, and one for size of the angle. For example:

    g.fillArc(10,10,100,100,0,90);

This draws a segment of a circle 100 by 100 pixels, with the top left corner of its bounding rectangle at 10,10. The segment starts at 3 o'clock and goes round to 12 o'clock. Two points about the angles:

● Arc angles are given in degrees (*whole* degrees, the parameters are **ints**), rather than the radians that are used in sine and cosine calculations.

● 0° is at 3 o'clock, and angles are measured counter-clockwise – use a negative value if you want to swing clockwise.

Here are some **drawArc()** and **fillArc()** statements at work:

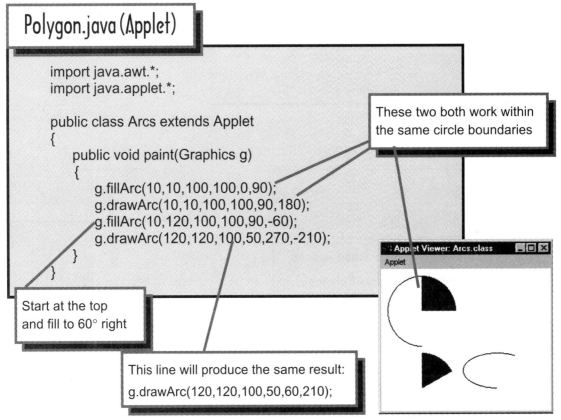

Polygon.java (Applet)

```
import java.awt.*;
import java.applet.*;

public class Arcs extends Applet
{
    public void paint(Graphics g)
    {
        g.fillArc(10,10,100,100,0,90);
        g.drawArc(10,10,100,100,90,180);
        g.fillArc(10,120,100,100,90,-60);
        g.drawArc(120,120,100,50,270,-210);
    }
}
```

These two both work within the same circle boundaries

Start at the top and fill to 60° right

This line will produce the same result:
g.drawArc(120,120,100,50,60,210);

Applet Viewer: Arcs.class
Applet

136

Pie charts

The next program again demonstrates arcs, but is also an example of working with arrays and shows another way to define colours. It takes a set of figures and displays them as a pie chart.

The arrays

There are three arrays, each of six elements (or as many as you like):

```
double[] value = new double[6];     // the figures to be charted
int[] slice = new int[6];           // the degrees in each slice
Color[] col = new Color[6];         // the colours of the slices
```

value must be a **double** or **float** type because of the calculations that are performed on its contents. Numbers are assigned to the *value* array in **init()**, and are then totalled, by running them through a loop:

```
for (int loop = 0; loop < 6; loop++)
    total+= value[loop];
```

If we divide each value by total, it gives us a fraction of the whole. Multiplying this by 360 converts it to degrees.

```
for (int loop = 0; loop < 6; loop++)
    slice[loop] = (int) (value[loop]/total*360);
```

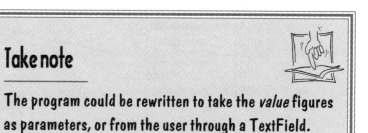

Take note

The program could be rewritten to take the *value* figures as parameters, or from the user through a TextField.

Predefined Colors

In the documentation for java.awt.Color you will find a set of thirteen predefined Color values. They are handy in situations like this, where you want a variety of colours, but aren't too bothered about the exact shades. To use them, write 'Color' followed by the name, e.g.

```
col[0] = Color.red;
```

The other names are: black, blue, cyan, darkGray, gray, green, lightGray, magenta, orange, pink, white and yellow.

PieCharts.java (Applet)

```java
import java.awt.*;
import java.applet.*;

public class PieCharts extends Applet
{
    double[] value = new double[6];
    int[] slice = new int[6];
    Color[] col = new Color[6];

    public void init()
    {
        double total = 0;

        value[0] = 1000;
        value[1] = 500;
        value[2] = 750;
        value[3] = 1200;
        value[4] = 300;
        value[5] = 1650;

        for (int loop = 0; loop < 6; loop++)
            total+= value[loop];
        for (int loop = 0; loop < 6; loop++)
            slice[loop] = (int) (value[loop]/total*360);

        col[0] = Color.red;
        col[1] = Color.green;
        col[2] = Color.blue;
        col[3] = Color.gray;
        col[4] = Color.magenta;
        col[5] = Color.yellow;
    }
    public void paint(Graphics g)
    {
        int start = 0;
        for (int loop = 0; loop < 6; loop ++)
        {
            g.setColor(col[loop]);
            g.fillArc(20,20,200,200,start,slice[loop]);
            start += slice[loop];
        }
    }
}
```

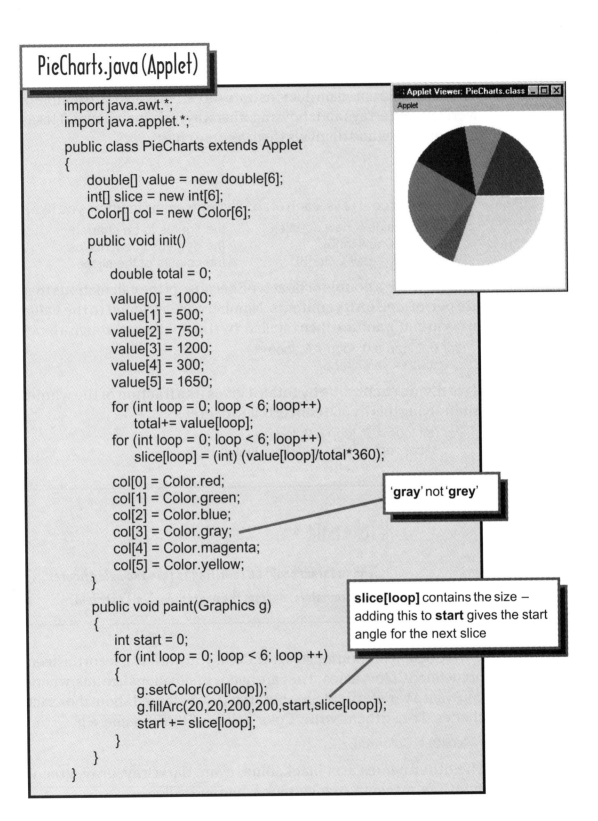

Applet Viewer: PieCharts.class
Applet

'**gray**' not '**grey**'

slice[loop] contains the size – adding this to **start** gives the start angle for the next slice

138

Painting on a Canvas

The next example, the longest in the book so far, ties together a number of the points covered in the last three chapters. It is a simple 'paint' program – and I do mean simple! The aim is to demonstrate ideas clearly, not to create a functional graphics application. It has a palette of six colours and a choice of three tools with which you can draw one item at a time. To make it into a working graphics tool you would need to store each item after drawing – either by saving the whole canvas image (difficult) or by adding them to an array of drawing instructions (complicated).

The applet uses a panelled layout, to the same pattern as the one in Layout3.java (page 125). The *tools* panel contains labelled buttons, arranged in a GridLayout. The *palette* panel also contains buttons, unlabelled but with coloured backgrounds, set in a GridLayout. The centre is taken by a redefined Canvas *drawarea*. Let's focus on that for a moment or two.

        class MyCanvas extends Canvas

This creates a new class, **MyCanvas**, which is a sub-class of the standard Canvas, and so shares all its properties, fields and methods.

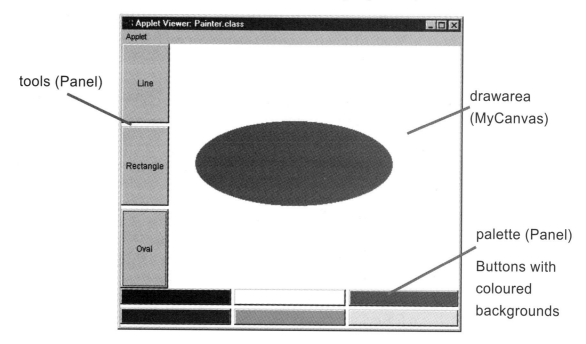

tools (Panel)

drawarea
(MyCanvas)

palette (Panel)

Buttons with
coloured
backgrounds

Within MyCanvas are the methods **mouseDown()**, **mouseDrag()** and **paint()**. These must be within MyCanvas because we want them to work on the *drawarea* object – if they were within the main program area they would work on the overall applet window.

There is also a fourth method:

```
public MyCanvas()
```

This is a *constructor*, a method called when an object is created by lines like this:

```
drawarea = new MyCanvas();
```

If you wanted to do anything when the object was set up, this is where you should write the code. As it happens, we don't, but there must always be a constructor method, with the same name as the class, in any class definition.

The rest of the program should need little explanation, as most of the techniques have been seen before.

Button clicks are picked up by action() and either set the *currentTool* value (0 = Line, 1 = Rectangle, 2 = Oval) or define the *currentColor*.

The **mouseDown()** and **mouseDrag()** methods are almost identical to those in Mouse1.java (page 93) – save yourself some typing and copy and paste them from there! When the mouse button is first pressed down, the start co-ordinates are collected into *mx* and *my*. As the mouse is dragged, the end co-ordinates are collected into *mx1* and *my1*, and the line, rectangle or oval is then drawn by a call to **paint()**.

In **paint()**, the *currentTool* value is used to select the drawing action. With **drawLine()**, the *mx, my, mx1, my1* co-ordinates are used directly to define the line:

```
if (currentTool == 0)
    g.drawLine(mx,my,mx1,my1);
```

fillRect() and **fillOval()** need the width and height values. These can be calculated from the start and end co-ordinates.

```
else if (currentTool == 1)
    g.fillRect(mx,my,mx1-mx,my1-my);
```

Painter.java (applet)

```java
import java.awt.*;
import java.applet.*;

public class Painter extends Applet
{
    Panel palette,tools;
    Button line,rect,oval;
    Button black,white,red,blue,green,yellow;
    MyCanvas drawarea;

    int mx = 0;
    int my = 0;
    int mx1 = 0;
    int my1 = 0;
    int currentTool = 0;
    Color currentColour = new Color(0,0,0);

    public void init()
        {
        setLayout(new BorderLayout());
        palette = new Panel();
        palette.setLayout(new GridLayout(2,3,5,5));
        black = new Button();
        black.setBackground(Color.black);
        white = new Button();
        white.setBackground(Color.white);
        red = new Button();
        red.setBackground(Color.red);
        blue = new Button();
        blue.setBackground(Color.blue);
        green = new Button();
        green.setBackground(Color.green);
        yellow = new Button();
        yellow.setBackground(Color.yellow);
        palette.add(black);
        palette.add(white);
        palette.add(red);
        palette.add(blue);
        palette.add(green);
```

Cursor positions

0 = line,1 = rect, 2 = oval

Starts set to black

Layout for applet

Layout for panel

```
            palette.add(yellow);
            add(palette, "South");

            tools = new Panel();
            tools.setLayout(new GridLayout(3,1,5,5));
            line = new Button("Line");
            rect = new Button("Rectangle");
            oval = new Button("Oval");
            tools.add(line);
            tools.add(rect);
            tools.add(oval);
            add(tools, "West");

            drawarea = new MyCanvas();
            add(drawarea,"Center");
            validate();
            }

    public  boolean action(Event evt, Object obj)
            {
            if(evt.target == line)
                currentTool = 0;
            if(evt.target == rect)
                currentTool = 1;
            if(evt.target == oval)
                currentTool = 2;
            if(evt.target == black)
                currentColour = new Color(0,0,0);
            if(evt.target == white)
                currentColour = new Color(255,255,255);
            if(evt.target == red)
                currentColour = new Color(255,0,0);
            if(evt.target == blue)
                currentColour = new Color(0,0,255);
            if(evt.target == green)
                currentColour = new Color(0,255,0);
            if(evt.target == yellow)
                currentColour = new Color(255,255,0);
            return true;
            }
```

Set **currentTool** – used in **paint()** to select the drawing method

Define **currentColour** – set later in **paint()**

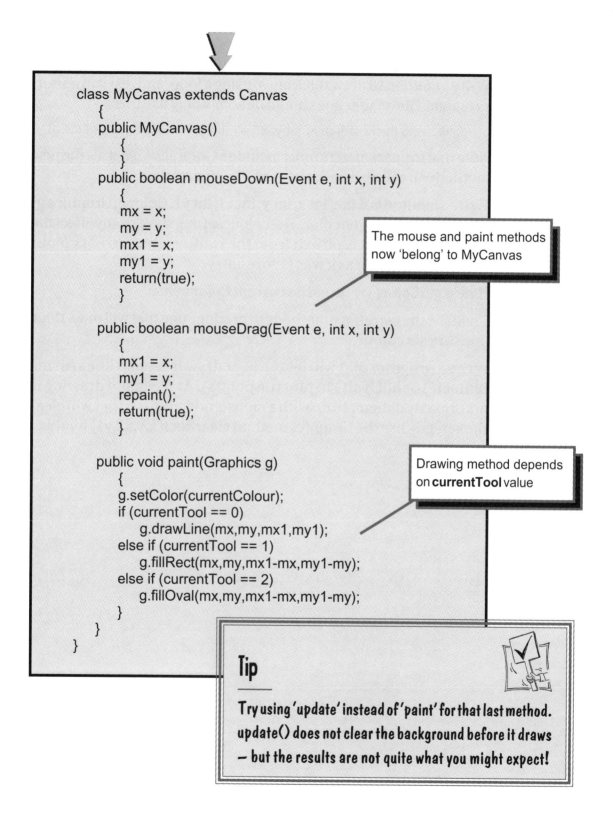

```
class MyCanvas extends Canvas
    {
    public MyCanvas()
        {
        }
    public boolean mouseDown(Event e, int x, int y)
        {
        mx = x;
        my = y;
        mx1 = x;
        my1 = y;
        return(true);
        }

    public boolean mouseDrag(Event e, int x, int y)
        {
        mx1 = x;
        my1 = y;
        repaint();
        return(true);
        }

    public void paint(Graphics g)
        {
        g.setColor(currentColour);
        if (currentTool == 0)
            g.drawLine(mx,my,mx1,my1);
        else if (currentTool == 1)
            g.fillRect(mx,my,mx1-mx,my1-my);
        else if (currentTool == 2)
            g.fillOval(mx,my,mx1-mx,my1-my);
        }
    }
}
```

The mouse and paint methods now 'belong' to MyCanvas

Drawing method depends on **currentTool** value

Tip

Try using 'update' instead of 'paint' for that last method. update() does not clear the background before it draws — but the results are not quite what you might expect!

Exercises

1 Write a method to draw thick lines, using a loop, and test it in a short program. The header line should be something like this:

```
public void thickLine(int x, int y, int x1, int y1, int width, Graphics g)
```

Note that the parameters must include a Graphics object, as the new method will call on drawLine() – a Graphics method.

2 Write a method **coLine(int x, int y, int x1, int y1, Color c, Graphics g)** to draw lines in a given color. The colour setting should only affect the lie being drawn – i.e. on exit from the routine, the current colour should be the same as it was before entry.

Hint: g.getColor() returns the current Color value.

3 Combine the two above methods to produce one that will draw thick lines in a set colour.

4 Write a program that will let the user draw freehand lines (using **fillRect()** or **fillOval()** to plot the points). As freehand drawing is notoriously difficult to do with a mouse, add a button that will clear the screen – use the Graphics method **clearRect(x,y,x1,y1)** for this.

7 Images, sounds and text

Image files

Like Web browsers, Java is designed to handle graphics files in two formats – GIF (including animated GIFs) and JPEG (with either a .JPEG or a .JPG extension). It cannot cope with the standard Windows formats BMP and PCX. If you want to create your own images, you will need a suitable graphics application, such as Paint Shop Pro. You can use this for drawing new images, or for converting pictures created in Paint – or almost anywhere else – into the GIF or JPEG formats.

As a general rule, you should use the GIF format in preference to JPEG. GIF files are significantly smaller, and therefore faster to load – an important consideration, especially where files have to be transferred over the World Wide Web. The main reason why JPEG files are larger is that they have palettes of 16.7 million colours, as opposed to the 256-colour palette of GIFs. Use JPEGs only where you need to show subtle variations of colour over a huge palette – and if the file is going up onto the Web, remember that many people will be viewing it on 256, or even 16-colour screens!

An animated GIF is a set of images, which are displayed in sequence, with a defined delay between each. They are used in exactly the same way as still images – the animation is entirely built into the image file, so all Java has to do is display it. The main things to remember here are that the files tend to be large, and that the animation speed is defined within the GIF. There are plenty of ready-made animated GIFs freely available on the Web – dig around in any shareware site and you should find lots – and if you want to create your own, go to Microsoft's site and pick up a copy of GIF Animator.

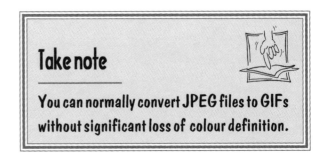

Take note

You can normally convert JPEG files to GIFs without significant loss of colour definition.

Using images

Images are easy to handle. They are stored in **Image** objects, with the files loaded into them by the **getImage()** method.

```
Image pic;
...
pic = getImage(getCodeBase(), "\images\car.gif");
```

getImage() takes as its parameter a URL – Uniform Resource Locator – the standard means of identifying a file anywhere on the Internet or in a computer.

URLs

The easiest way to handle the URL is with **getCodeBase()**. This works out the URL of the directory in which the program is stored. If the image file is in the same directory, then you would simply follow it up with the filename:

```
getCodeBase(), "car.gif"
```

If the file is in a sub-directory, you also need to add its name, as in the example above, where *car.gif* is in the *images* sub-directory.

The great thing about the **getCodeBase()** approach is that it will give the right URL when the files are on your system and when they are uploaded to your Web space on your access provider's server.

If the image file is stored in a completely different place from the code, then you will have to define the URL using the **java.net.URL** class. This throws an exception that you must catch (see page 76). For example, if you wanted to use an image from your access provider's store:

```
import java.net.*;
...
try{
    pic = getImage(new URL("http://www.net.co/images/ukflag.gif"));
}
catch(MalformedURLException e)
{}
```

The address is written in full, then converted to a URL object. The **catch** block might get an alternative image from a more secure source.

Displaying images

Images can be displayed directly on the applet, or in a canvas, using the **drawImage()** method. At its simplest, it takes this form:

```
g.drawImage(pic, 0, 0, this);
```

The image *pic* is drawn at its natural size, with the top left corner at 0,0. *this* refers to the window or canvas in which the image is being drawn. The method needs to know which object to update as it is scaling or converting the image.

The second common form of the method has two extra parameters to set the width and height – if these are different from the original.

```
g.drawImage(pic, 0, 0, 100, 50, this);
```

The image will be drawn 100 pixels wide by 50 high.

Image1.java pulls these methods together in a simple demonstration.

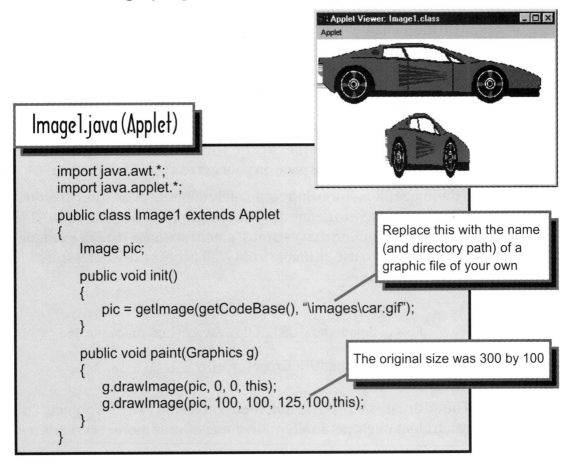

Image1.java (Applet)

```
import java.awt.*;
import java.applet.*;

public class Image1 extends Applet
{
    Image pic;

    public void init()
    {
        pic = getImage(getCodeBase(), "\images\car.gif");
    }

    public void paint(Graphics g)
    {
        g.drawImage(pic, 0, 0, this);
        g.drawImage(pic, 100, 100, 125,100,this);
    }
}
```

Replace this with the name (and directory path) of a graphic file of your own

The original size was 300 by 100

Simple animation

As long as the image is small, and you don't want to do anything else in the applet, you can produce simple animation by moving the image, controlling its speed with a delay loop. With larger images, which take longer to load and to draw, or where you want to run the animation alongside other activities, you must use threads (see Chapter 8). This next example bounces a ball across the screen.

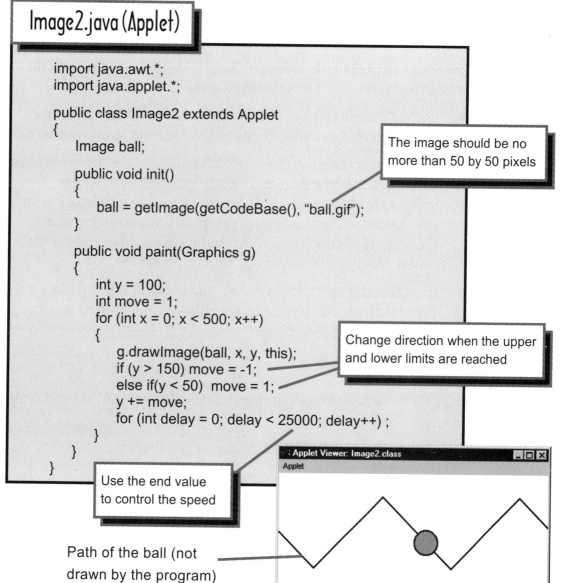

Image2.java (Applet)

```java
import java.awt.*;
import java.applet.*;

public class Image2 extends Applet
{
    Image ball;

    public void init()
    {
        ball = getImage(getCodeBase(), "ball.gif");
    }

    public void paint(Graphics g)
    {
        int y = 100;
        int move = 1;
        for (int x = 0; x < 500; x++)
        {
            g.drawImage(ball, x, y, this);
            if (y > 150) move = -1;
            else if(y < 50)  move = 1;
            y += move;
            for (int delay = 0; delay < 25000; delay++) ;
        }
    }
}
```

The image should be no more than 50 by 50 pixels

Change direction when the upper and lower limits are reached

Use the end value to control the speed

Path of the ball (not drawn by the program)

Applet Viewer: Image2.class
Applet

149

Image filters

If you check out the documentation for the java.awt.image package, you will find that it contains several interfaces and classes that can be used for manipulating images. The next program dips into these to create cropped and enlarged images. It displays an image – I have used a map – and when the mouse is clicked anywhere on it, it displays an enlarged view of the area around the mouse.

The interfaces

Interfaces act as links between objects and classes, providing them with extra facilities. There are three in the image class:

- **ImageConsumer** is the object which takes the data for a new image after it has been processed. We are not using one here.

- **ImageObserver** is the object which monitors the progress of an image as it is being drawn. These are mainly used where images are being prepared off-screen, for use in animation. In this, as in the previous Image programs, we are using one – though it is not obvious. The drawImage parameter this tells Java to use the image as its own ImageObserver.

- **ImageProducer** is the source of data for an image. In this program we load one image from file, and use that as the source for a second image.

The classes and methods

ImageFilter brings in methods for changing the colour, size and scale of image objects.

CropImageFilter is an extension of ImageFilter that crops a rectangular section out of an image.

```
ImageFilter imgF = new CropImageFilter(cropX, cropY,420,330);
```

This line defines the ImageFilter object *imgF* as one which takes a block 420 x 330 pixels, starting at *cropX*, *cropY*. Where it takes it from is not defined at this stage.

FilteredImageSource forms the link between the source image and the ImageFilter object, with the output depending upon the nature of the ImageFilter. Here, the line:

ImageProducer imgP = new FilteredImageSource(source.getSource(), imgF);

crops the area defined in *imgF* out of the *source* image. This is then converted from an ImageProducer object to a standard image by:

crop = createImage(imgP);

Before you start...

The program below was designed to work with an image 840 x 660 pixels, and a display area of 420 x 330 – half scale. All the calculations are based on those values, so if your image is a different size, you will have to vary the numbers to suit.

If you want to simplify things a bit, you can omit the limit checks in **Cropper()** – this output will be a bit messier, but it won't hurt to go beyond the limits of the original image.

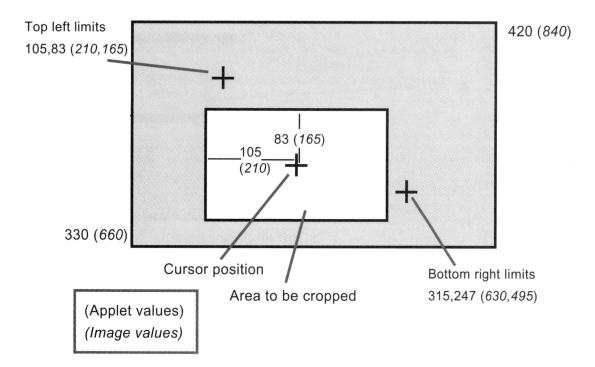

Top left limits
105,83 *(210,165)*

420 *(840)*

83 *(165)*

105
(210)

330 *(660)*

Cursor position

Area to be cropped

Bottom right limits
315,247 *(630,495)*

(Applet values)
(Image values)

```
import java.awt.*;
import java.awt.image.*;
import java.applet.*;

public class Image3 extends Applet
{
    Image source;
    Image crop;
    boolean cropped = false;

    public void init()
    {
    source = getImage(getCodeBase(), "map.gif");
    }

    public boolean mouseDown(Event e, int x, int y)
    {
        if (cropped == false)
        {
            Cropper(x,y);
            cropped = true;
        }
        else
            cropped = false;

        repaint();
        return(true);
    }

    public void Cropper(int x, int y)
    {
        if (x <105)
            x = 105;
        if (x > 315)
            x = 315;
        if (y < 83)
            y = 83;
        if (y > 247)
            y = 247;
```

Download this GIF from the Made Simple site, or create your own

A click either crops the image or sets the display back to to full size

Updates the display

The limit checks are optional, but produce a neater result

```java
        int cropX, cropY;

        cropX = 2 * x - 210;
        cropY = 2 * y - 165;
        ImageFilter imgF = new CropImageFilter(cropX, cropY,420,330);
        ImageProducer imgP
            = new FilteredImageSource(source.getSource(), imgF);
        crop = createImage(imgP);
    }

    public void paint(Graphics g)
    {
        if (cropped)
            g.drawImage(crop,0,0,420,330,this);
        else
            g.drawImage(source,0,0,420,330,this);
    }
}
```

The screen's x,y co-ordinates are converted to image co-ordinates – subtracting 210 and 165 gives the top left corner of the crop area

This is all one line

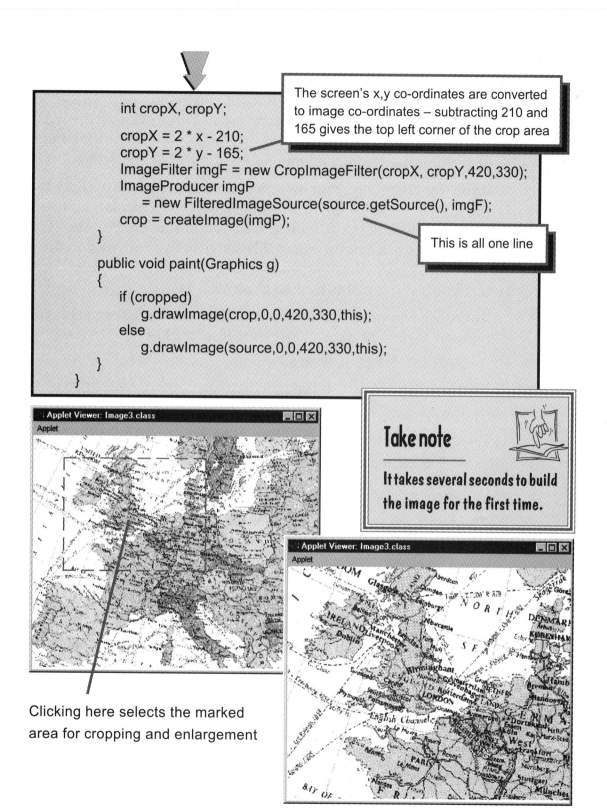

Take note

It takes several seconds to build the image for the first time.

Clicking here selects the marked area for cropping and enlargement

Sounds

Java can currently handle sound files only in the **au** audio clip format developed by Sun. This is a bit limiting, as Windows uses the WAV format, but all is not lost. For testing purposes, you can use the au files in the Audio folders of the JumpingBox and TicTacToe demos.

If you want to record your own messages and music, Cool Edit, by David Johnson, will convert WAV files (and other formats) into au sounds. CoolEdit is available from all good shareware sites – try **www.shareware.com** for a start. When converting the files, you must set the options to 8 bit μlaw, and set the sample rate to 8000 Hz. This is the only version of au that Java can play.

There are two ways to play sounds. The simplest uses the play() method, taking as its parameter the URL of the file:

```
play(getCodeBase(), "ding.au");
```

That loads and plays the file immediately.

The alternative is to set up an AudioClip object, load the file into there, and then play it later in the program:

```
AudioClip beeper;
...
beeper = getAudioClip(getCodeBase(), "beep.au");
```

This approach gives you more control as you now have access to the three AudioClip methods – **play()**, **loop()** and **stop()**.

```
beeper.play();      // plays the clip once
beeper.loop();      // plays the clip repeatedly
beeper.play();      // stops both loop or single play
```

The example program use the beep.au and ding.au files from the TicTacToe/Audio folder. They are not very special, but at least they are there! If you copy them into your java files folder, the URLs will be much simpler to write.

When the applet runs, you will hear a continuous beeping and see two buttons. Clicking "Press for service" will load and run the 'ding' file; clicking "Stop that beeping!" will give you some peace.

Sound1.java (Applet)

```java
import java.awt.*;
import java.applet.*;

public class Sound1 extends Applet
{
    AudioClip beeper;
    Button ringer;
    Button quiet;

    public void init()
    {
    beeper = getAudioClip(getCodeBase(), "beep.au");
    ringer = new Button("Press for service");
    add(ringer);
    quiet = new Button("Stop that beeping!");
    add(quiet);
    beeper.loop();
    }

    public boolean action(Event e, Object obj)
    {
    if (e.target == ringer)
        play(getCodeBase(), "ding.au");
    if (e.target == quiet)
        beeper.stop();
    return true;
    }
}
```

Load *beep.au* into the **beeper** AudioClip

Set **beeper** playing continuously

Load and play *ding.au* once

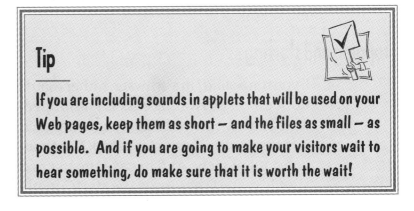

Tip

If you are including sounds in applets that will be used on your Web pages, keep them as short — and the files as small — as possible. And if you are going to make your visitors wait to hear something, do make sure that it is worth the wait!

155

Sound control

Sound1 is a fine example of the cheap and cheerful approach to programming – it's short and it works, in a limited fashion, as long as everything is OK. But if you are sending a program out into the big wide world, where anything can happen, some refinements are needed.

Checking the file

What happens if the sound file is not where it is supposed to be, or fails to reach the user? Neither the **play(URL)** nor the **getAudioClip()** method return error reports if they cannot find the file – the program just carries on soundlessly. This may be acceptable. If it isn't, there is a solution – but it is not a very tidy one.

The basic problem is that you can create a URL to a non-existent file and few of the URL-using methods complain! One which will throw an exception is **openStream()**. To use this, we must first create the URL as an object, and then try to open a stream (a link to a file) to it.

```
try{
mytuneUrl = new URL(getCodeBase(), "mytune.au");
inst = mytuneUrl.openStream();
}
catch(MalformedURLException e) {}
catch(IOException e)
{ message = "Failed to find sound file";  }
```

The **new URL(...)** line throws the **MalformedURLException** – which does not test that it actually exists – and that must be caught, though you can't do anything with it. **openStream()** throws the **IOException** and it is in its **catch** block that we write the code to respond to a missing file.

Stopping and starting

If you run *Sound1* in a browser, rather than the AppletViewer, you may notice a very irritating effect. The looped sound continues to play after you have moved off the page containing the applet! The solution is to turn it off in the applet's **stop()** method that runs when the applet goes out of view. And in case the user returns to the applet, you should restart the loop in the **start()** method.

Sound2.java (Applet)

```java
import java.awt.*;
import java.applet.*;

public class Sound2 extends Applet
{
    AudioClip mytune;
    boolean playing = false;

    public void init()
    {
    try{
        mytuneUrl = new URL(getCodeBase(), "mytune.au");
        inst = mytuneUrl.openStream();
        }
        catch(MalformedURLException e) {}
        catch(IOException e)
        { message = "Failed to find sound file"; }

        mytune = getAudioClip(mytuneUrl);
        mytune.loop();
        playing = true;
    }
    public void start()
    {
        if (playing)
            mytune.loop();
    }

    public void stop()
    {
        if (playing)
            mytune.stop();
    }
    public void paint(Graphics g)
    {
        g.drawString(message,0,30);
        g.setFont(new Font("SanSerif",Font.BOLD,30));
        g.drawString("Welcome to my world",50,50);
    }
}
```

> playing is true when loop() is active

> Check that the file is there

> Indicates that loop() is active

> **(playing)** is the same as **(playing == true)**

> The loop has been stopped, but **playing** is still true

Text layout

If you want to place text accurately, the **FontMetrics** methods will give you the height, width and other measurements, of text written in a given font. The example below creates a **FontMetrics** object *metrics*, which is linked to **Font** *f*. It uses the methods **getHeight()** to set the vertical spacing between lines, and **stringWidth()** to find the width of each string. If a string will fit on the line after an existing one, it is placed there, otherwise, it is displayed on the next line.

I've designed the program to take its text and font size as parameters, to make experimentation easier. They could be written directly into the applet if you prefer.

Fonts1.java (Applet)

```java
import java.awt.*;
import java.applet.*;

public class Fonts1 extends Applet
{
    Font f;
    FontMetrics metrics;
    int fsize;
    int textHeight;
    int textWidth;
    String[] text = new String[4];

    public void init()
    {
        text[0] = getParameter("line0");
        text[1] = getParameter("line1");
        text[2] = getParameter("line2");
        text[3] = getParameter("size");
        fsize = Integer.parseInt(text[3]);
        f = new Font("Serif",0,fsize);
        metrics = getFontMetrics(f);
        resize(400,250);
    }
```

new FontMetrics(f) would not work – FontMetrics is an abstract class, and you cannot create an object directly from it

resize(x,y) sets the window size – overriding the width and height passed from the applet

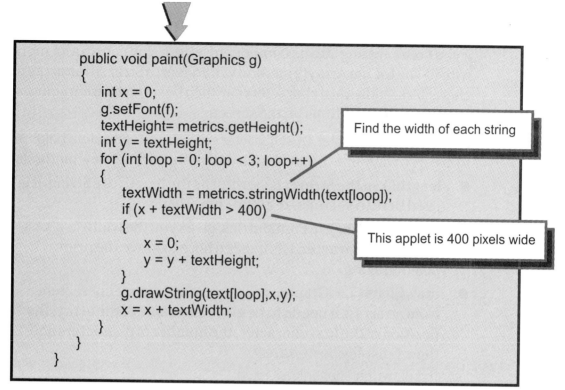

```
public void paint(Graphics g)
{
    int x = 0;
    g.setFont(f);
    textHeight= metrics.getHeight();
    int y = textHeight;
    for (int loop = 0; loop < 3; loop++)
    {
        textWidth = metrics.stringWidth(text[loop]);
        if (x + textWidth > 400)
        {
            x = 0;
            y = y + textHeight;
        }
        g.drawString(text[loop],x,y);
        x = x + textWidth;
    }
}
```

Find the width of each string

This applet is 400 pixels wide

Here are the matching HTML parameters:

```
<PARAM NAME = line0 VALUE = "Java Made Simple">
<PARAM NAME = line1 VALUE = " - or at least made simpler">
<PARAM NAME = line2 VALUE = "...but don't expect">
<PARAM NAME = line3 VALUE = " miracles">
<PARAM NAME = size VALUE = 30>
```

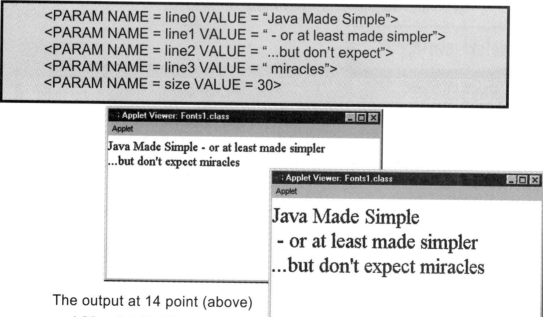

The output at 14 point (above)
and 30 point (right)

Strings and arrays

If you break a String into its component letters, you can do a lot more with it. The **toCharArray()** method will convert a String to an array of characters – individual characters can then be set in different colours, fonts, sizes, or positions on the screen.

In the WaveText applet, the characters are placed at random heights, to create a wavy line of text. Watch out for three other new methods:

- **length()**, in the **String** class, returns the length of a String. It is used here to set the size of the char[] array.

- **getCharWidth()**, in **FontMetrics**, gives you the width in pixels of a single character. It is needed here to move the print position along.

- **drawChars()**, in Graphics, displays one or more characters from an array. It needs to be given the name of the array, the position of the first character, the number of characters and the x,y display position. e.g.

      g.drawChars(letter,loop,1,x,y);

  This uses the *letter[ ]* array – give the name alone, without [ ] – and displays the one character at *loop*.

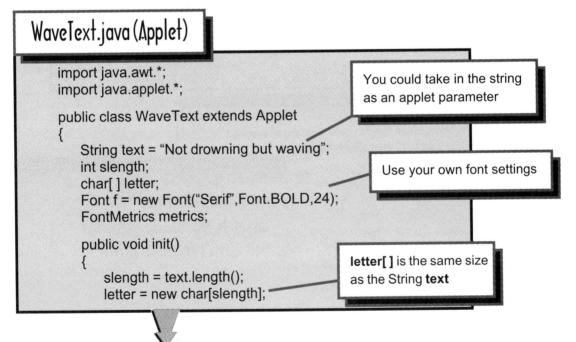

WaveText.java (Applet)

```
import java.awt.*;
import java.applet.*;

public class WaveText extends Applet
{
    String text = "Not drowning but waving";
    int slength;
    char[ ] letter;
    Font f = new Font("Serif",Font.BOLD,24);
    FontMetrics metrics;

    public void init()
    {
        slength = text.length();
        letter = new char[slength];
```

You could take in the string as an applet parameter

Use your own font settings

letter[ ] is the same size as the String **text**

160

```
        letter = text.toCharArray();
        metrics = getFontMetrics(f);
}

public boolean mouseDrag(Event e, int x, int y)
{
    repaint();
    return true;
}

public void paint(Graphics g)
{
    int x, y;
    g.setFont(f);
    x = 0;
    y = 50;
    for (int loop = 0; loop < slength; loop++)
    {
        g.drawChars(letter,loop,1,x,y);
        x+= metrics.charWidth(letter[loop]);
        y = 50 + (int)((java.lang.Math.random()*20) - 10);
    }
}
}
```

When the mouse is dragged, the text waves

Moves the print position along for the width of the current character

Produces a value in the range of 50 +/- 10

Applet Viewer: WaveText.class

Applet

Not dr°w^ning b_ut wa_ving

Applet started.

Tip

Setting a different colour for each letter will also produce a striking effect — even more so if you wave it around at the same time.

161

Exercises

1   Design and write a simple 'jigsaw' applet. It should have an array, holding a set of images which form a picture when moved into the right places. To create the pieces, take a picture and cut it into equal size pieces, saving each as a GIF. If the names are in a series, e.g. "pic0.gif", "pic1.gif", "pic2.gif", etc, you will be able to generate their names as you run through the loop to load the files. The name-making line will look something like this:

```
name = "pic" + loop + ".gif"
```

Pieces should be moved to their new positions dragging with the mouse. You do not need to use **mouseDrag()** for this – simply find the place of the piece at **mouseDown()**, and its target place at **mouseUp()**.

2   Write an applet which will roll the characters in a string, shifting each one to the left and bringing the first round to the end of the string. The rolling should be repeated until the characters are back in their original places.

Hints: Include a delay if you want to see anything!

Clear old text off the drawing area before displaying the characters again, or you will get a nasty blur!

8 Threads

Threads

Threads are sequences of code that can be executed independently alongside one another. A simple applet can only do one thing at a time, but one that contains threads can do several things at once.

Threads are essential for good animation, and even for simple animation if you don't want to bring the rest of the applet to a halt.

If you have any time-consuming tasks to do – such as downloading images or other files – handling them through a thread will allow you to do something else to keep your viewers happy while they wait.

Threaded applets

The simplest way to include a Thread in a program is to implement the **Runnable** interface. This handles the **run()** method, which holds all the Thread's code. The addition of **implements Runnable** to the **class** line brings in the interface:

```
public class Counter extends Applet implements Runnable
```

The Thread is declared at class level, but set to null. When **start()** is executed, an instance is created and the *Thread's* **start()** method is called. This then calls **run()**, to execute the Thread code.

```
Thread timer = null;
...
timer = new Thread(this);
timer.start();
```

In **run()**, there is first a check to see if the Thread is active – if the user leaves and returns to the applet, **start()** will be excuted, and you do not want to try to create a second instance.

```
while (timer != null)
```

If it is, the Thread waits for a second, updates a counter and repaints the display.

```
try
{Thread.sleep(1000);}
    catch (InterruptedException e){}
count++;
repaint();
```

The **sleep()** method – it works in milliseconds, so 1000 = 1 second. This feature of the Thread class is invaluable for animation – it only suspends the Thread, leaving the rest of the program active.

In **stop()**, the Thread is turned off:

```
timer = null;
```

This is so that it also stops execution when the user leaves the applet. And of course, it it is restarted by **start()**. This is not essential in this case – the Thread could be left running without interfering with anything else, or coming to any harm.

mouseDrag() is nothing to do with the Thread. It is there simply to show that the rest of the program can be doing active things while the Thread is running. This one lets you drag a string around the screen.

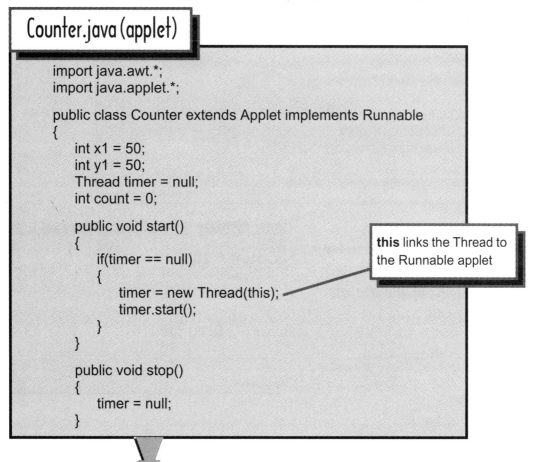

Counter.java (applet)

```java
import java.awt.*;
import java.applet.*;

public class Counter extends Applet implements Runnable
{
    int x1 = 50;
    int y1 = 50;
    Thread timer = null;
    int count = 0;

    public void start()
    {
        if(timer == null)
        {
            timer = new Thread(this);
            timer.start();
        }
    }

    public void stop()
    {
        timer = null;
    }
```

this links the Thread to the Runnable applet

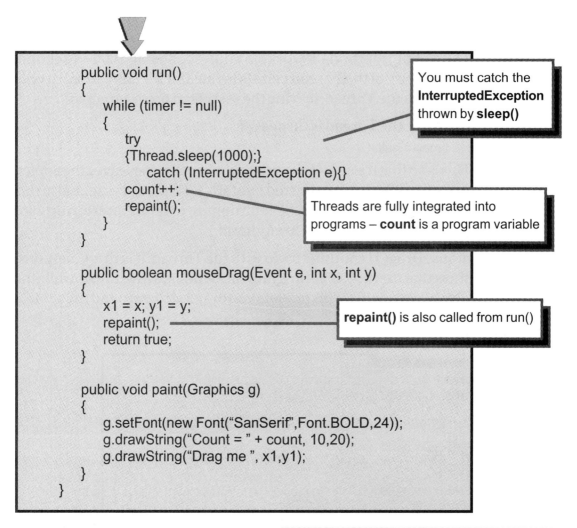

```
public void run()
{
    while (timer != null)
    {
        try
        {Thread.sleep(1000);}
            catch (InterruptedException e){}
        count++;
        repaint();
    }
}

public boolean mouseDrag(Event e, int x, int y)
{
    x1 = x; y1 = y;
    repaint();
    return true;
}

public void paint(Graphics g)
{
    g.setFont(new Font("SanSerif",Font.BOLD,24));
    g.drawString("Count = " + count, 10,20);
    g.drawString("Drag me ", x1,y1);
}
}
```

You must catch the **InterruptedException** thrown by **sleep()**

Threads are fully integrated into programs – **count** is a program variable

repaint() is also called from run()

The count display is updated every second, no matter what else happens. Dragging on the text also updates the screen.

Applet Viewer: Counter.class

Applet

Count = 20

Drag me

Applet started.

166

Animated images

The hardest part to animation is not in writing the code – that's the easy bit – but in creating the images. If you are light on artistic talent, stick to simple pictures – like I do!

This program animates a set of three images of an old jalopy, moving it across the screen and backfiring as it goes. Here are the images:

redcar0.gif   redcar1.gif   redcar2.gif

The images are stored in the *pic[]* array, with the subscript of the one to be displayed held by *current*. This is cycled through the values 0 to 2 by the lines:

```
current++;
if (current >2)
    current = 0;
```

The technique can be extended for as large an array as you need.

The movement is simply straight across screen, with the x position incrementing by 10 each time.

The image is changed and moved every 1/10th of a second – faster would be smoother, but smoothness is not wanted here – with the timing controlled by a **sleep(100)** instruction.

Experiment to find you how far and how fast to move your images.

Animation is improved by sound effects, so add those if possible. The AudioClip should be loaded into an object, if it will be reused, but could be loaded and played directly if it is a one-off. (Look back to page 154 for more on the sound methods.)

The Thread is set up and used to the same pattern as in the last program – you could even use *Counter.java* as a basis for this one.

Animate1.java (applet)

```java
import java.awt.*;
import java.applet.*;

public class Animate1 extends Applet implements Runnable
{
    int x;
    Thread animator = null;
    Image[] pic = new Image[3];
    int current = 0;
    AudioClip bang;

    public void init()
    {
        pic[0] = getImage(getCodeBase(), "redcar0.gif");
        pic[1] = getImage(getCodeBase(), "redcar1.gif");
        pic[2] = getImage(getCodeBase(), "redcar2.gif");
        bang = getAudioClip(getCodeBase(), "bang.au");
    }

    public void start()
    {
        if(animator == null)
        {
            animator = new Thread(this);
            animator.start();
        }
    }

    public void stop()
    {
        animator = null;
    }

    public void run()
    {
        while (animator != null)
        {
            x+= 10;            // move it along
            if (x > 400) x = 0; // back to start
            current++;
```

> If you have a large array, generate the filenames in a loop (see the solution to Exercise 7.1 on page 188)

> Add a sound if wanted

> Start and stop the thread on entry to and exit from the applet.

```
            if (current == 2)
                bang.play();
            if (current >2)
                current = 0;    //cycle through the images
            repaint();
            try
            {Thread.sleep(100);} catch (InterruptedException e){}
        }
    }

    public void paint(Graphics g)
    {
        g.drawImage(pic[current],x,100,this);
    }
}
```

> Don't forget to catch the **InterruptedException**

It looks more impressive
when it is moving!

Take note

If you have more than a couple of images, or if they are
large ones, you should build a MediaTracker-based Thread
loading routine into your program. The next few pages
show you how to do this.

Controlled loading

If you have tried to use any large images, you will have noticed that Java load slowly and builds up the image in stages. This is messy – and avoidable. (Though you can't get around the slowness!)

The **MediaTracker** methods will allow you to monitor the progress of incoming images, and if you set this inside a Thread, the rest of the program can be doing something useful while it waits for the images. At the very least, you can display a "Loading" message, then replace it with the completed image in one movement.

Here's the Image3.java 'cropping' applet, rewritten to use this loading technique. The new material is picked out in bold in the full listing so that you can see what to add. This is how it works.

MediaTracker

The MediaTracker is essentially a list of incoming files with methods for adding files to the list, and for checking when they are fully loaded. An instance should be declared at class level:

```
MediaTracker track;
```

It is then created in **init()**, and – after the downloading has been started by **getImage()** – the file is added to the list.

```
track = new MediaTracker(this);
source = getImage(getCodeBase(), "map.gif");
track.addImage(source,0);
```

addImage() takes two parameters – the name of the image and an ID number to identify it on the list. There is only one image on this list, but it must be numbered, and it may as well be 0.

Within the Thread's **run()**, we use **waitForID(0)** to suspend execution until the image with the ID 0 is fully loaded. The method throws an InterruptedException which must be caught – though you don't have to do anything with it.

```
try {
    track.waitForID(0);
    } catch (InterruptedException e) { }
```

If you were loading an array, or other set, of images, you could use this to hold execution until a particular image was loaded, or wait for the whole set to load with:

```
track.waitForAll();
```

waitForID() and **waitForAll()** do not check that the images have been loaded properly. This shouldn't matter too much if you are reasonably sure that the files are present and the communications are good. If you do want to check for errors, the test:

```
if(track.isErrorID(0)) ...
```

will be true if there was an error during loading.

MediaTracker also has other methods for checking the status and progress of incoming images – look them up in the help pages for the java.awt set.

The Thread and the loaded variable

The Thread is set up in exactly the same way as in the previous programs in this set. Its **run()** method only has one real job, which is to wait for the image to load. After that, it sets the *loaded* variable to true, calls for a **repaint()** and exits.

loaded is needed to control the screen display. Its state determines whether to show the "Loading please wait" message, or the image.

```
if (loaded == false)
    g.drawString("Loading please wait",0,50);
else
{
    if (cropped)
        ...
```

You could, of course, replace the simple message with a more colourful title screen – created with text and drawn objects, not images!

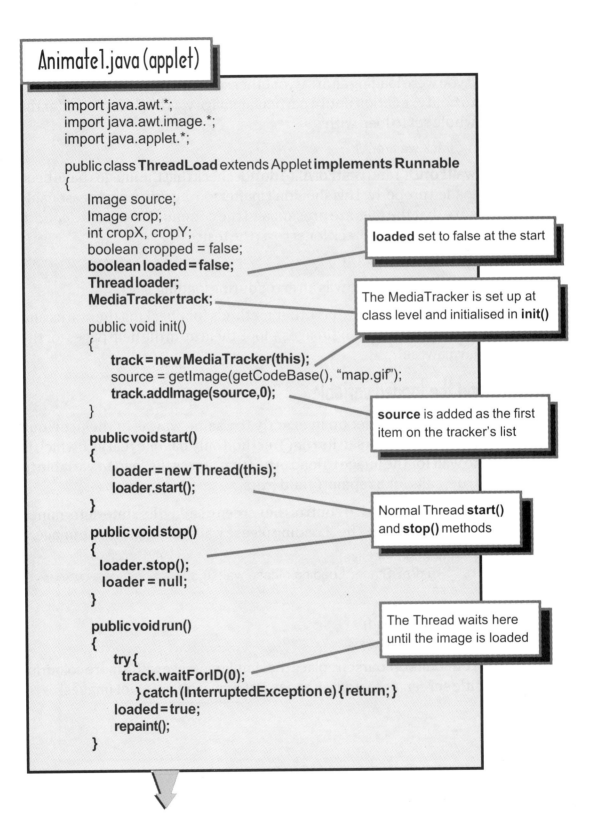

Animate1.java (applet)

```java
import java.awt.*;
import java.awt.image.*;
import java.applet.*;

public class ThreadLoad extends Applet implements Runnable
{
    Image source;
    Image crop;
    int cropX, cropY;
    boolean cropped = false;
    boolean loaded = false;
    Thread loader;
    MediaTracker track;

    public void init()
    {
        track = new MediaTracker(this);
        source = getImage(getCodeBase(), "map.gif");
        track.addImage(source,0);
    }
    public void start()
    {
        loader = new Thread(this);
        loader.start();
    }
    public void stop()
    {
        loader.stop();
        loader = null;
    }

    public void run()
    {
        try {
            track.waitForID(0);
            } catch (InterruptedException e) { return; }
        loaded = true;
        repaint();
    }
```

loaded set to false at the start

The MediaTracker is set up at class level and initialised in init()

source is added as the first item on the tracker's list

Normal Thread start() and stop() methods

The Thread waits here until the image is loaded

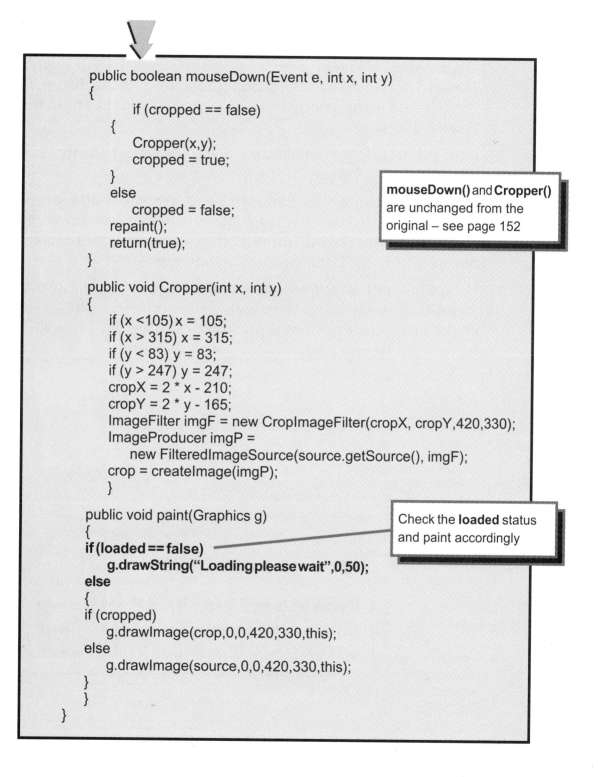

```
public boolean mouseDown(Event e, int x, int y)
{
        if (cropped == false)
    {
        Cropper(x,y);
        cropped = true;
    }
    else
        cropped = false;
    repaint();
    return(true);
}

public void Cropper(int x, int y)
{
    if (x <105) x = 105;
    if (x > 315) x = 315;
    if (y < 83) y = 83;
    if (y > 247) y = 247;
    cropX = 2 * x - 210;
    cropY = 2 * y - 165;
    ImageFilter imgF = new CropImageFilter(cropX, cropY,420,330);
    ImageProducer imgP =
        new FilteredImageSource(source.getSource(), imgF);
    crop = createImage(imgP);
    }

public void paint(Graphics g)
{
if (loaded == false)
    g.drawString("Loading please wait",0,50);
else
{
if (cropped)
    g.drawImage(crop,0,0,420,330,this);
else
    g.drawImage(source,0,0,420,330,this);
}
}
}
```

mouseDown() and Cropper() are unchanged from the original – see page 152

Check the **loaded** status and paint accordingly

Exercises

1 Adapt *MoveText.java* (page 98), to run the animation through a Thread. The active part of the existing program – the lines that move the ball – are in the paint() method. Where should they be in the Threaded version?

   Hint: The delay loop should be replaced by a **sleep()**, and that can only be done in a Thread.

2 Take the bouncing ball animation (Image 2.java, page 149) and turn that into a Threaded applet. When you have the movement successfully controlled by the Thread, you might then like to adapt the program further to bring the loading under Thread control.

3 Using Counter.java as a base, develop a program that will draw a target – a rectangle or oval – on screen at random intervals. If the user clicks on it, before the next is drawn, count it as a hit, otherwise increment a misses counter.

Tip

If you want to develop your Java skills and knowledge further, try *Java: a Practical Approach*, by Neil Fawcett and Terry Ridge, published by Butterworth-Heinemann.

9 Answers to exercises

Chapter 1

1   This is simply practice in using the **javac** and **java** utilities. The program contains only println statement.

```
class Address
{
    public static void main(String[] args)
    {
        System.out.println("Jumbo Butterpat");
        System.out.println("The Green Gnome");
        System.out.println("Little Moaning");
        System.out.println("Dribble Valley");
    }
}
```

2   It is possible to calculate the size of text, so that you can position it accurately (see Chapter 7), but trial and error will also get you there! Allow 15 to 20 pixels between lines.

```
import java.applet.Applet;
import java.awt.Graphics;

public class AddressApp extends Applet
{
    public void paint(Graphics g)
    {
        g.drawString("Jumbo Butterpat", 100, 20);
        g.drawString("The Green Gnome", 89, 40);
        g.drawString("Little Moaning", 116, 60);
        g.drawString("Dribble Valley", 116, 80);
    }
}

<HTML>
<HEAD>
  <TITLE> Address Applet  </TITLE>
</HEAD>
<BODY>
<P>Here's my address:</P>
<P><APPLET CODE="AddressApp.class" WIDTH=200 HEIGHT=120>
</APPLET></P>
<P>Please write</P>
</BODY>
</HTML>
```

Chapter 2

1   The calculation needed here is **age = 365 * year + 30 * month + day.**

```
class Ex21
{
public static void main(String[ ] args)
{
    int day = 12;        // age in days, months and years
    int month = 3;
    int year = 48;

    int age;

    age = 365 * year + 30 * month + day;

    System.out.println("You are " + age + " days old");
    }
}
```

2   This follows the same pattern as the last. The 2-digit year format will work up until the Year 2000. After that, you will need 4-digit years.

```
class Ex22
{
public static void main(String[ ] args)
{
    int bday = 5;        // birthday
    int bmonth = 4;
    int byear = 49;
    int day = 17;        // today's date
    int month = 7;
    int year = 97;

    int birthday, today, age;

    birthday = 365 * byear + 30 * bmonth + bday;
    today = 365 * year + 30 * month + day;
    age = today - birthday;

    System.out.println("You are " + age + " days old");
    }
}
```

3   This combines the techniques from the InString.java (page 51) and Buffer.java (page 52) programs. You have to remember to append a space between the words to stop them running into each other.

```
class Ex23
{
    public static void main(String[ ] args)
    {
        String firstArg;
        String secondArg;
        StringBuffer s1 = new StringBuffer("You entered ");

        firstArg = args[0];
        secondArg = args[1];
        s1.append(firstArg);
        s1.append(" ");                    // space between the words
        s1.append(secondArg);
        System.out.println(s1);
    }
}
```

Chapter 3

1   As each line contains one more than the previous, the value of the outer loop should be used as the end test for the inner loop.

```
class Ex31
{
    public static void main(String[] args)
    {
    int  outer;
    int  inner;

    for (outer = 1; outer <= 10 ; outer++)
        {
        for (inner = 1; inner <= outer; inner++)
            System.out.print("*");
        System.out.println();
        }
    }
}
```

2   If you want really big loops, use a **long** for the count.

```
class Ex32
{
    public static void main(String[] args)
    {
    long    count = 0;
    System.out.println("Starting to count");
    while (count < 500000)
        {
        count++;
        }
    System.out.println("Done");
    }
}
```

3   The trick here is to realise that, if x is the random number and num[] the array, num[x]++ increments the matching element.

```
class Ex33
{
    public static void main(String[] args)
    {
    int[] num = new int[10];
    int loop, x;
```

```
        for (loop = 0; loop < 10; loop++)
            num[loop] = 0;
        for (loop = 0; loop < 1000; loop++)
            {
            x = (int)(java.lang.Math.random() * 10);
            num[x]++;
            }
        for (loop = 0; loop < 10; loop++)
            System.out.println(loop + "occurrences " + num[loop]);
        }
    }
```

4   I've generated a random character in the range 0 to 128. You could
     also use the **System.in.read()** method (page 40).

```
class Ex34
{
    public static void main(String[] args)
    {
    char    letter;
    do
    {
    letter = (char)(java.lang.Math.random() * 128);
    if (letter < ' ')
        System.out.println("Non-printing");
    else if ((letter >= 'a') && (letter <= 'z'))
        System.out.println(letter + "Lower case");
    else if ((letter >= 'A') && (letter <= 'Z'))
        System.out.println(letter + "Upper case");
    else if ((letter >= '0') && (letter <= '9'))
        System.out.println(letter + "Digit");
    else
        switch (letter)
        {
            case '.':System.out.println("Full stop");
            case ',':System.out.println("Comma");
            case '$':System.out.println("Dollar");
            case '~':System.out.println("Tilde");
            default :System.out.println("Some other symbol");
        }
    }
    while(letter != 'q');
    }
}
```

Chapter 4

1   In my program the colour fades from black, through shades of grey by
     increasing the red, green and blue components together. You could
     make it fade out one colour at a time by using three nested loops, one
     for each colour.

```
import java.awt.*;
import java.applet.*;

public class Ex41 extends Applet
{
    int shade;
    Font sansbold = new Font("Helvetica",Font.BOLD,24);

    public void paint(Graphics g)
    {
        for (shade = 0; shade < 256; shade++)
        {
        g.setFont(sansbold);
        g.setColor(new Color(shade,shade,shade));
        g.drawString("Fading away", 0, 30);
        for (int delay = 0; delay < 25000; delay++)
            ;
        }
    }
}
```

2   Set the HEIGHT to 400, in the HTML page for this applet.

```
import java.awt.*;
import java.applet.*;

public class Ex42 extends Applet
{
    int size = 24;

    public boolean mouseDown(Event e, int x, int y)
    {
        if (y < 200) size++;
        if (y > 200) size--;
        repaint();
        return(true);
    }
```

```
        public void paint(Graphics g)
        {
            g.setFont(new Font("Helvetica",Font.BOLD,size));
            g.drawString("This font is " + size + " point", 0, 200);
        }
    }
```

3   There's lots of room for individual variation here. This is my solution. It is designed to run in a window 500 x 400, and with HTML code that contains the line:

```
<PARAM NAME = myname VALUE = "your name goes here">
```

Make use of Copy and Paste to create those random() lines!

```
import java.awt.*;
import java.applet.*;

public class Ex43 extends Applet
{
    String name;

    public void init()
    {
        name = getParameter("myname");
    }

    public void paint(Graphics g)
    {
        g.setFont(new Font("Helvetica",Font.BOLD, 48));
        for (int loop = 0; loop < 200; loop++)
        {
            int x = (int)(java.lang.Math.random() * 500);
            int y = (int)(java.lang.Math.random() * 400);
            int red = (int) (java.lang.Math.random() * 255);
            int green = (int) (java.lang.Math.random() * 255);
            int blue = (int) (java.lang.Math.random() * 255);
            g.setColor(new Color(red,green,blue));
            g.drawString("*", x, y);
        }
        g.drawString(name,50,200);
    }
}
```

Chapter 5

1   At first, just get this working so that it changes the colour of the rectangle, then add the lines to enable and disable the buttons.

```
import java.awt.*;
import java.applet.*;

public class Ex51 extends Applet
{
    Button butRed, butBlue, butGreen;

    Color red = Color.red;            //defined in java.awt.Color
    Color blue = Color.blue;
    Color green = Color.green;
    Color current = red;              // start with Red

    public void init()
    {
        butRed = new Button("Red");
        butRed.setEnabled(false);     // so Red is turned off
        butBlue = new Button("Blue");
        butGreen = new Button("Green");
        add(butRed);
        add(butBlue);
        add(butGreen);
        validate();     // make sure components are added properly
    }

    public boolean action(Event e, Object arg)
    {
        Object target = e.target;
        if (target == butRed)     // Turn on blue and green
        {
            butRed.setEnabled(false);
            butBlue.setEnabled(true);
            butGreen.setEnabled(true);
            current = red;
        }
        if (target == butBlue)     // Turn on red and green
        {
            butRed.setEnabled(true);
            butBlue.setEnabled(false);
            butGreen.setEnabled(true);
            current = blue;
        }
```

```
            if (target == butGreen)      // Turn on red and blue
            {
                butRed.setEnabled(true);
                butBlue.setEnabled(true);
                butGreen.setEnabled(false);
                current = green;
            }
            repaint();
            return true;
        }

        public void paint(Graphics g)
        {
            g.setColor(current);
            g.fillRect(100,50,200,100);
        }
    }
```

2   As you need to generate a random point when the applet first starts,
     and when the New Game button is pressed, it makes sense to write the
     code as a method – I've called it **hide()**.

     Trying to hit a pixels is incredibly difficult. You must allow your
     players a bit of latitude. The solution here is to find the absolute
     difference between the guess and the target centre, for both the x and
     y co-ordinates, and count it a hit if the total difference is less than 10.

```
import java.awt.*;
import java.applet.*;

public class Ex52 extends Applet
{
    int rX, rY;
    Button newgame;
    boolean found;
    String feedback = "Where is it?";

    public void init()
    {
        newgame = new Button("New Game");
        add(newgame);
        hide();
    }
```

```
    public void hide()
    {
        rX = (int)(java.lang.Math.random()*500); // applet Width
        rY = (int)(java.lang.Math.random()*500); // applet Height
        found = false;
    }

    public boolean action(Event e, Object arg)
    {
        if (e.target == newgame)
            hide();
        return true;
    }

    public boolean mouseDrag(Event e, int x, int y)
        {
        int missed;
        missed = java.lang.Math.abs(x - rX) + java.lang.Math.abs(y - rY);
        feedback = "Missed by " + missed;
        if (missed < 10)
        {
            feedback = "Found it";
            found = true;
        }
        repaint();
        return true;
    }

    public void paint(Graphics g)
        {
        g.drawString(feedback, 10,10);
        if (found)
            g.drawOval(rX-5,rY-5,10,10);
        }
}
```

3   The new components all follow existing patterns in the way they are created and used. Use the *bold* button and code as a model for the *italic* (remember that the Font.ITALIC value is 2), and *Serif* as a model for the new font. You will need a Panel with a GridLayout(2,1) to take the Label and Canvas.

The listing for this is at the Java Made Simple page at **www.bh.com**.

Chapter 6

1   This is not a perfect solution! As the loop is on the **y** values, the closer
a line is to vertical, the less it is thickened. If we looped on the **x** values,
the thickening would not work well on more horizontal lines. A better
solution would have both loops, and select which to use by the test:

```
if (x1 - x) > (y1 - y)
```

```java
import java.applet.*;
import java.awt.*;

public class Ex61 extends Applet
{
    public void paint(Graphics g)
    {
        thickLine(20,20,120,120,6,g);
        thickLine(20,20,20,120,4,g);
    }
    public void thickLine(int x, int y, int x1, int y1, int width, Graphics g)
    {
        for (int loop = 0; loop < width; loop++)
            g.drawLine(x, y+loop, x1,y1+loop);
    }
}
```

2   Store the current colour in **Color temp** before using **setColor()**!

```java
import java.applet.*;
import java.awt.*;

public class Ex62 extends Applet
{
    Color red = new Color(255,0,0);
    public void paint(Graphics g)
    {
        coLine(20,20,20,120,red,g);
        g.drawLine(20,20,120,20);
    }
    public void coLine(int x, int y, int x1, int y1, Color c, Graphics g)
    {
        Color temp = g.getColor();
        g.setColor(c);
        g.drawLine(x, y, x1, y1);
        g.setColor(temp);
    }
}
```

4   After you have got this working, you might like to combine the drawing routine and Clear button into the Painter program.

The clearRect() values are set to wipe an applet 500 x 500.

```java
import java.applet.*;
import java.awt.*;

public class Ex63 extends Applet
{
    int x1 = 0;
    int y1 = 0;
    Button clear;
    boolean wipe = false;

    public void init()
    {
        clear = new Button("Clear Screen");
        add(clear);
    }

    public boolean action(Event e, Object o)
    {
        wipe = true;
        repaint();
        return true;
    }

    public boolean mouseDrag(Event e, int x, int y)
    {
        x1 = x;
        y1 = y;
        repaint();
        return true;
    }

    public void update(Graphics g)
    {
        if (wipe == true)
        {
            g.clearRect(0,0,500,500);   // applet size
            wipe = false;
        }
        else g.fillRect(x1, y1,2,2);
    }
}
```

Chapter 7

1   Here's one solution. It uses an image 600 * 480, overall, divided into 9 pieces, each 200 * 160. The numbers are all based on these sizes.

At **mouseDown()**, the number of the clicked piece is stored in *pick*. At **mouseUp()**, *drop* takes that of the new place. The two are then swapped.

```java
import java.awt.*;
import java.awt.image.*;
import java.applet.*;

public class Ex71 extends Applet
{
    Image[] piece = new Image[9];
    int[] x = new int[9];
    int[] y = new int[9];
    Image temp;
    int pick, drop;

    public void init()
    {
        int loop,rand;
        String name;
        for (loop = 0; loop < 9; loop++)
        {
            name = "MAT" + loop + ".gif";
            piece[loop] = getImage(getCodeBase(), name);
            x[0] = 0; y[0] = 0;
            x[1] = 201; y[1] = 0;
            x[2] = 402; y[2] = 0;
            x[3] = 0; y[3] = 161;
            x[4] = 201; y[4] = 161;
            x[5] = 402; y[5] = 161;
            x[6] = 0; y[6] = 322;
            x[7] = 201; y[7] = 322;
            x[8] = 402; y[8] = 322;
        }
        for (loop = 0; loop < 9; loop++)
        {
            rand = (int) (java.lang.Math.random()*9);
            temp = piece[rand];
            piece[rand] = piece[loop];
            piece[loop] = temp;
        }
        repaint();
    }
```

> The files are named **MAT0.gif**, **MAT1.gif**, **MAT2.gif**, etc. This line forms the names

> Shuffle the pieces, swapping each with a random other

188

```
public boolean mouseDown(Event e, int x, int y)
{
    pick = (int) (x/200) + (int) (y/160) * 3;
    return(true);
}

public boolean mouseUp(Event e, int x, int y)
{
    drop = (int) (x/200) + (int) (y/160) * 3;
    temp = piece[drop];
    piece[drop] = piece[pick];
    piece[pick] = temp;
    repaint();
    return(true);
}

public void paint(Graphics g)
{
for (int loop = 0; loop < 9; loop++)
    g.drawImage(piece[loop], x[loop], y[loop],200,160,this);
}
}
```

You could add code in **mouseDrag()** to move the selected piece

The pieces are laid in a grid (0–1–2, 3–4–5, 6–7–8). This turns the x,y values into the piece number

The display using the MAT series of images. You can get these from the Java Made Simple page at:
http://www.bh.com

189

2   The first half of this program is almost identical to WaveText.java. To roll the string, the first letter is copied into temp, then each element in the array takes the letter from the next – until the one before the end. The last letter is copied back in from temp. The whole loop is repeated for as many times as there are letters, to give one full roll.

```java
import java.awt.*;
import java.applet.*;

public class Ex72 extends Applet
{
    String text = "What goes around, comes around";
    int slength;
    char[] letter;
    Font f = new Font("Serif",Font.BOLD,24);

    public void init()
    {
        slength = text.length();
        letter = new char[slength];
        letter = text.toCharArray();
    }

    public void paint(Graphics g)
    {
        char temp;
        g.setFont(f);
        for (int repeat = 0; repeat < slength; repeat++)
        {
            g.clearRect(0,0,400,100);
            g.drawChars(letter,0,slength,0,50);
            temp = letter[0];
            for (int loop = 0; loop < slength-1; loop++)
            {
                letter[loop] = letter[loop + 1];
                for (int delay = 0; delay < 10000; delay++) ;
            }
            letter[slength-1] = temp;
        }
    }
}
```

Chapter 8

1   The Thread follows the normal pattern, but notice that the moving loop has been transferred into **run()**. I've used **update()**, rather than **paint()**, as it gives slightly smoother animation.

```java
import java.awt.*;
import java.applet.*;

public class Ex81 extends Applet implements Runnable
{
    String text, temp;
    int speed;
    int x;
    Thread mover = null;

    public void init()
    {
        text = getParameter("message");        // null checks removed
        temp = getParameter("speed");          // to save space
        speed = Integer.parseInt(temp);
    }

    public void start()
    {
        if(mover == null)
        {
            mover = new Thread(this);
            mover.start();
        }
    }

    public void stop()
    {
        mover = null;
    }

    public void run()
    {
        while (mover != null)
        {
        for ( x = 200; x > 0; x—)
            {
            repaint();
            try {Thread.sleep(speed);} catch (InterruptedException e){}
            }
        }
    }
}
```

```
public void update(Graphics g)
{
    g.setFont(new Font("SanSerif",Font.BOLD,24));
    g.clearRect(x,80,300,30);
    g.setColor(new Color(0,0,0));
    g.drawString(text, x, 100);
}
}
```

2   If you succeeded with Exercise 8.1, you should have no trouble with
this. It uses the standard Thread pattern, and again has the movement
routines in **run()**. **paint()** here does no more than draw the image.

```
import java.awt.*;
import java.applet.*;

public class Ex82 extends Applet implements Runnable
{
    int x,y;
    Thread bouncer = null;
    Image ball;

    public void init()
    {
        ball = getImage(getCodeBase(), "ball.gif");
    }

    public void start()
    {
        if(bouncer == null)
        {
            bouncer = new Thread(this);
            bouncer.start();
        }
    }

    public void stop()
    {
        bouncer = null;
    }

    public void run()
    {
        while (bouncer != null)
        {
            y = 100;
            int move = 1;
```

```
                    for (x = 0; x < 500; x++)
                    {
                        repaint();
                        if (y > 150) move = -1;
                        else if(y < 50) move = 1;
                        y += move;
                        try {Thread.sleep(10);}
                            catch (InterruptedException e){}
                    }
                }
            }
        public void paint(Graphics g)
        {
            g.drawImage(ball, x, y, this);
        }
    }
```

3   The tricky bit in this program is how and when you record hits and
     misses. If it is done solely within **mouseDown()**, it would be possible
     to get several hits at once by repeatedly clicking on the target – and
     a miss would not be counted if you did not click before the target was
     redrawn. Using the Boolean variable *ontarget*, we can record – once
     only – when the target it hit, and failure to click also counts as a miss.

```
import java.awt.*;
import java.lang.Math;
import java.applet.*;

public class Ex83 extends Applet implements Runnable
{
    int tx, ty;
    int hits = 0;
    int misses = 0;
    boolean ontarget = false;
    Thread target = null;

    public void start()
    {
        if(target == null)
        {
            target = new Thread(this);
            target.start();
        }
    }
}
```

```java
public void stop()
{
    target = null;
}
public void run()
{
    int delay;
    while (target != null)
    {
        if (ontarget) hits++;
        else misses++;
        ontarget = false;
        repaint();
        delay = (int)(Math.random() * 2000)+ 500;
        try
        {Thread.sleep(delay);} catch (InterruptedException e){}
    }
}
public void paint(Graphics g)
{
    g.drawString("Hits: " + hits + " Misses: " + misses, 10,20);
    tx = (int)(Math.random()*400);
    ty = (int)(Math.random()*400);
    g.fillOval(tx, ty, 20,20);
}
public boolean mouseDown(Event e, int x, int y)
{
    if((x > tx && x < tx+20) && (y > ty && y < ty+20))
        ontarget = true;
    return true;
}
}
```

Take note

The text files of these solutions, as well as those of the larger examples elsewhere in the book, and their related graphics, are available from the Made Simple Programming pages at:

http://www.bh.com

Index